Isaac Hernández | **Difference Makers**
PORTRAITS OF LEADERS IN THE ARTS, SOCIAL JUSTICE AND SUSTAINABILITY

PUBLISHING BY THE SEAS

Publishing by the Seas, Inc., 1187 Coast Village Rd. Suite 1-530, Santa Barbara, CA 93108
www.publishingbytheseas.com

Difference Makers
Copyright 2014 © by Isaac Hernández and Nancy Black/Mercury Press International
Photography: Copyright 2014 © by Isaac Hernández/ IsaacHernandez.com
All rights reserved. No part of this book may be used or reproduced by any means, graphic, electronic, or mechanical, including photocopying, recording, taping, or by any information storage retrieval system without written permission except in the case of brief quotations embodied in critical articles and reviews.

Cataloging-in-Publication Data is on file with the Library of Congress.

ISBN: 978-1-940654-97-3

Design: Helena Hernández Herrero

First Edition
April 2014

Isaac Hernández | Difference Makers
PORTRAITS OF LEADERS IN THE ARTS, SOCIAL JUSTICE AND SUSTAINABILITY

WORDS BY NANCY BLACK

Publishing by the Seas
Santa Barbara, California

INDEX

FOREWORD AND ACKNOWLEDGEMENTS   6

PHOTOGRAPHS

The Arts
AMY TAN	8
GORE VIDAL	10
ISABEL ALLENDE	12
LENORE KANDEL	14
ANTONIO BANDERAS	16
JAVIER BARDEM	18
WILL SMITH	20
RAMÓN SENDER BARAYÓN	22

Social Justice
ARCHBISHOP DESMOND TUTU	24
INA MAY GASKIN AND STEPHEN GASKIN	26
JODIE EVANS	28
MELISSA K. NELSON	30
MICHAEL ROSSMAN	32
NANCY KOPPELMAN	34
OSCAR CARMONA	36
ROBIN LIM, CPM	38
VICKI POLLACK	40
WAVY GRAVY	42
ZAINAB SALBI	44

Sustainability
ANDY LIPKIS	46
BUD BOTTOMS	48
HAROLD POWELL	50
JUDY GOLDHAFT AND PETER BERG	52
LARRY SALTZMAN AND LINDA BUZZELL SALTZMAN	54
MARC MCGINNES	56
MICHAEL POLLAN	58
NINA SIMONS AND KENNY AUSUBEL	60
PAOLO SOLERI	62
PAUL EHRLICH	64
PAUL RELIS	66
ROBERTA SALAZAR	68
SELMA RUBIN	70
SYLVIA EARLE	72

PHOTOGRAPHER'S BIO   74

"Never doubt that a small group of thoughtful, committed citizens can change the world. Indeed, it's the only thing that ever has."

— Margaret Mead

THANK YOU

I am daily grateful for the world I live in and for those who work to make it a better place. I've been fortunate to interview and photograph people who, in my eyes, are contributing to that world profoundly.

These are my Difference Makers, the ones that inspire me to become a better person, the ones I think of when I'm stuck or feeling sad. They play in three areas which are close to my heart: art, social justice and sustainability.

I would need another book to be able to name all the amazing people who have made a difference to me personally. Some stand out, including my family, friends, and the students I've been fortunate to teach theater, photography and art.

Many helped in making this book possible. Carlos Fresneda, US Bureau Chief for *El Mundo* (Spain), was my editor and partner for most of these photo sessions. Nancy Black not only wrote the profiles, but also worked behind the scenes to make these portraits a reality. Helena Hernández turned a collection of photos into a beautiful book, and Patricia Selbert with Erika Römer of Publishing by the Seas had faith in the project and made the book happen.

Thank you to all who have assisted in this production (whether you know it or not), including Quike Hernández, David Gala, Alejandro Andreatta, Jorge Torres, Kelly Webster, Ramón Sender Barayón, Ana Reymundo, Rosana Ubanell, Carol Marshall, Maureen McFadden, Pablo Scarpellini, and the great people at *El Mundo* and Bioneers.

Thank you all. This is also your creation.

Isaac Hernández

Dedicated to the memory of
Peter Berg, Stephen Gaskin, Lenore Kandel, Michael Rossman, Selma Rubin, Paolo Soleri and Gore Vidal

FOREWORD AND ACKNOWLEDGEMENTS

DIFFERENCE MAKERS

A community of individual sparks can light a global fire for what's possible. This series of portraits by Isaac Hernández brings together powerhouse people influencing a variety of fields, from local leaders to internationally-known figures. They share a universal calling to contribute for a positive shift, for which they have each found unique expressions. We all know Difference Makers. You probably are one, too.

I think everyone aspires to contribute. Most people do that every day, unsung, and with little fanfare. This collection of inspiring leaders is an ongoing work, an open investigation of contribution. For every Difference Maker included here, there are countless unmentioned. This book is a ballad for all, represented by this small selection. It has been a delight to compile and edit the words to briefly summarize what these incredible leaders are up to.

These portraits were taken to accompany interviews, published in different international publications, including *El Mundo*, a Spanish national newspaper and international website. They are part of an ongoing passion project, spanning a decade.

By publishing this series of interviews in the media, and now with this book, we aim to shine a spotlight on impactful actions for a healthy, empowered and sustainable future. Please donate to them, volunteer, or use their examples to craft and inspire your own great projects for thriving.

Isaac has the special gift of putting his subjects at ease. His talent and unique vision have been inspiring me since we met in 1991; I was so smitten I married him, over twenty years ago. It's my deepest joy to share this collaboration of words and images for inspiration. We offer them up with love.

Nancy Black

"Everyone must dream. We dream to give ourselves hope. To stop dreaming - well, that's like saying you can never change your fate. Isn't that true?"

AMY TAN
Storyteller

Novelist Amy Tan has written numerous bestsellers, including *The Joy Luck Club, Saving Fish from Drowning, The Opposite of Fate: A Book of Musings, The Kitchen God's Wife, The Hundred Secret Senses*, and *The Bonesetter's Daughter*. She has also written *Sagwa, The Chinese Siamese Cat*, a children's book. And she just published her latest novel, *The Valley of Amazement*, after what she calls "six years of anxiety."

She is a proud member of the Rock Bottom Remainders, a rock band consisting of published writers, including Barbara Kingsolver, Matt Groening, Dave Barry and Stephen King, among others. Together, they have fun raising money for literacy.

She lives with late-stage neuroborreliosis, known as Lyme Disease, and supports The Lyme Disease Association, raising funds for this and other good causes. Her words gift billions of readers, worldwide.

www.lymediseaseassociation.org
www.amytanauthor.com
www.rockbottomremainders.com

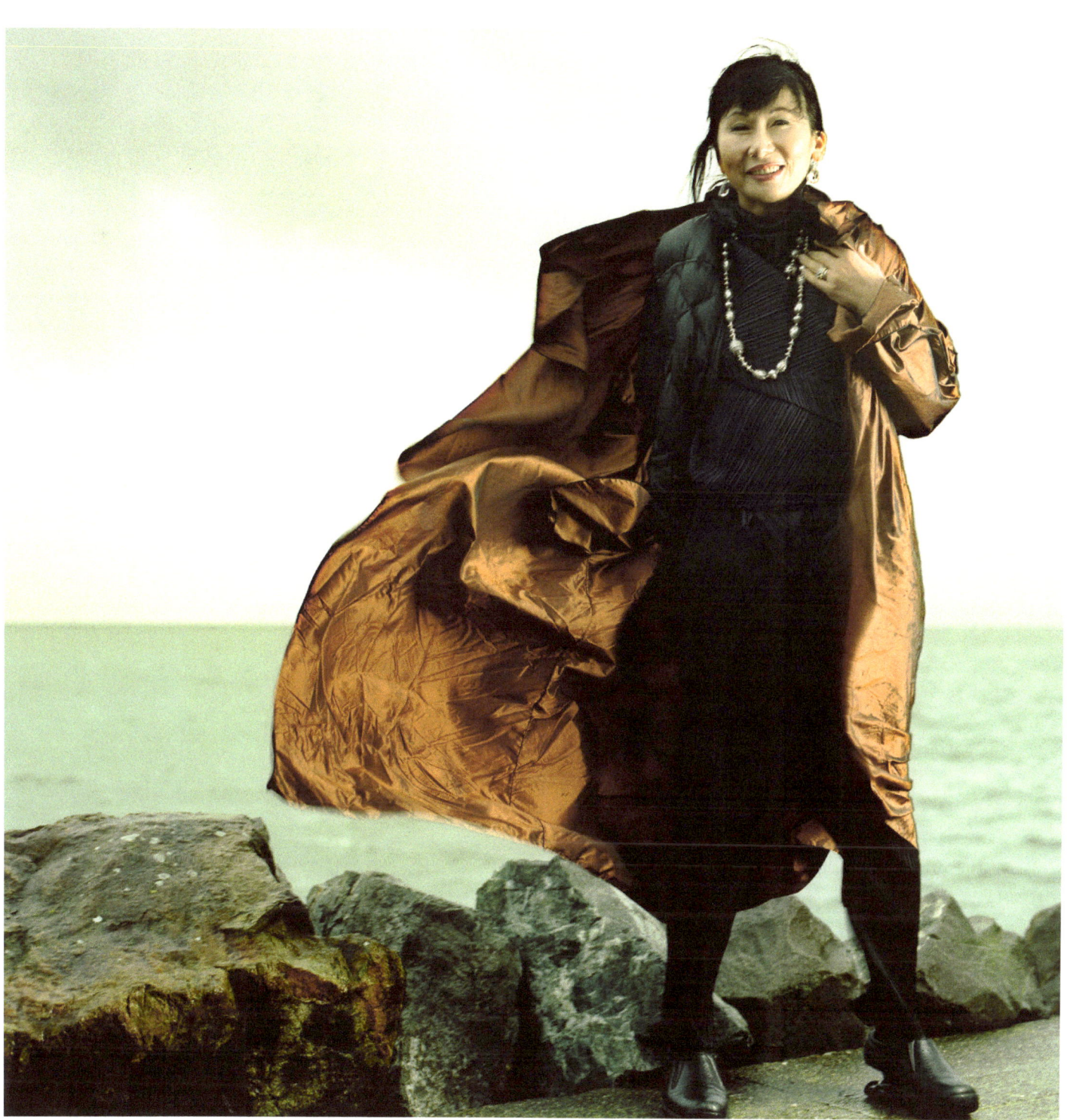

"'Liberal' comes from the Latin 'liberalis', which means 'pertaining to a free man'. In politics, to be liberal is to want to extend democracy through change and reform. One can see why that word had to be erased from our political lexicon."

GORE VIDAL
Novelist, screenwriter, playwright, writer, politician

Norman Mailer told the author of *Myra Breckenridge* (1968), "No one can accuse you of not being able to turn a good line," after years of public feuding. Mailer called Vidal one of the "great writers of the 20th century, and as clever with words as all get out."

Gore Vidal was famous for challenging social dictates, beginning with the ground-breaking novel *The City and the Pillar* (1948), which outraged critics for featuring open homosexuality. Vidal argues that "although our notions about what constitutes correct sexual behavior are usually based on religious texts, those texts are invariably interpreted by the rulers in order to keep control over the ruled."

For six decades, Gore Vidal applied himself to a wide variety of sociopolitical, sexual, historical, and literary themes, with more than 20 novels, eight plays, 13 screenplays, and over 200 essays as a writer with *The Nation, the New Yorker, New Statesman, the New York Review of Books* and *Esquire*, including the critically lauded *Palimpsest: A Memoir*. Vidal's *United States (Essays 1952-1992)*, which won the 1993 National Book Award.

His grandfather served as Democratic senator from Oklahoma, which contributed to Gore Vidal's political philosophy, critical of foreign and domestic policies shaped by American imperialism. Vidal ran for a seat in the US Congress for upstate New York in 1960 (losing narrowly), and for the California Senate in 1982, losing in the primary to Jerry Brown.

Vidal was a member of the advisory board of the World Can't Wait organization. He passed away on July 31, 2012, at the age of 86.

www.worldcantwait.org

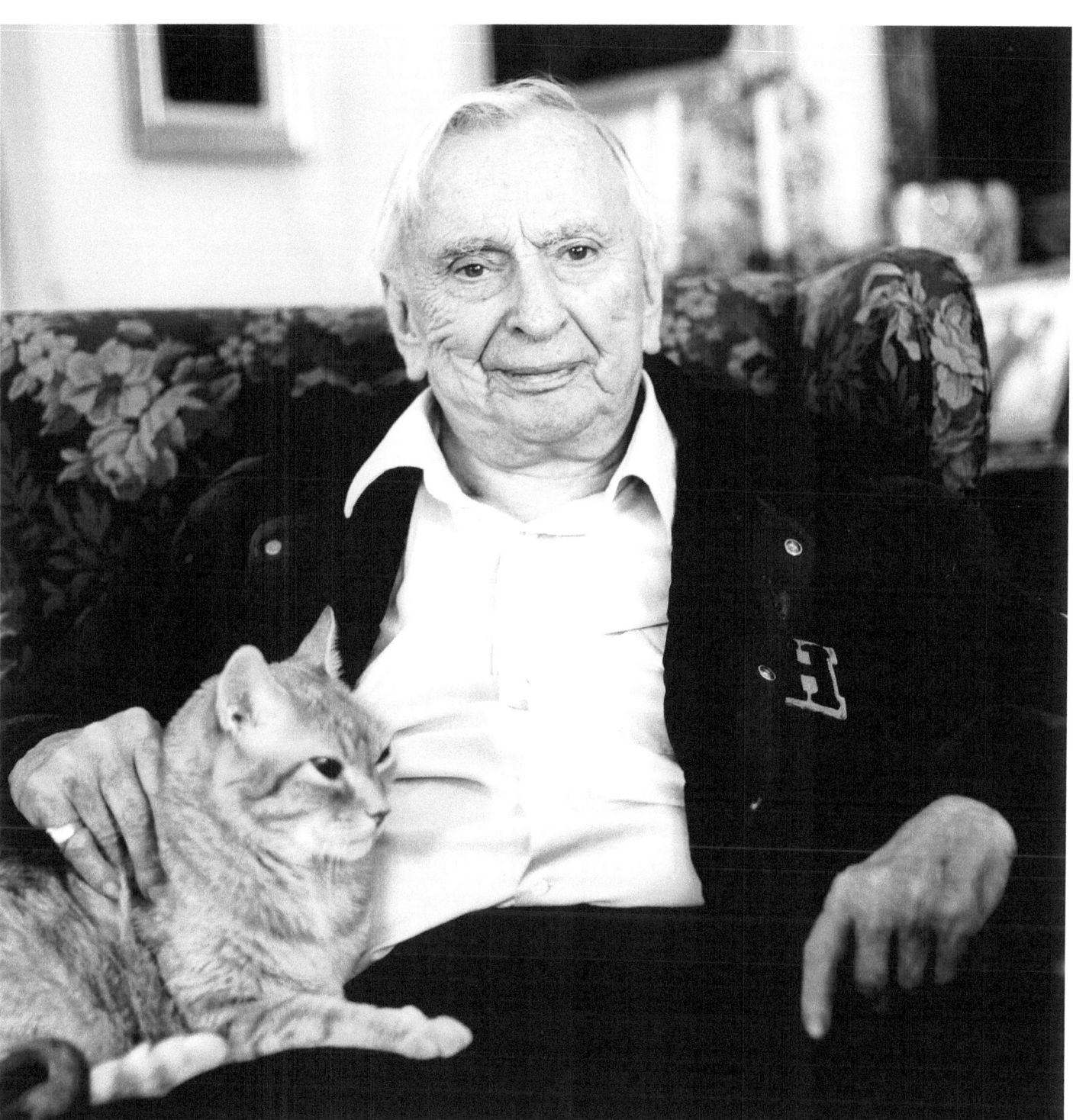

"Fear is inevitable, I have to accept that, but I cannot allow it to paralyze me."

ISABEL ALLENDE
Writer, founder of the Isabel Allende Foundation

When Chilean author Isabel Allende wrote *The House of the Spirits* in her little kitchen, she never suspected she would end up writing 20 books, selling more than 57 million copies in 35 languages. Or that she would receive 12 international honorary doctorates and 50 awards. However, she says her most significant achievements are not her books, "but the love I share with a few people—especially my family—and the ways in which I have tried to help others."

For over two decades she has lectured internationally about women's rights and the empowerment of women, politics, Chile, the creative process, spirituality, and her own work.

She created The Isabel Allende Foundation to empower women and girls worldwide, in memory of her daughter, Paula Frías, who died at the age of 28. Allende contributes to the foundation with income from the sale of her books.

Paula worked as a volunteer in poor communities of Venezuela and Spain. When in doubt, she would ask, "What is the most generous thing to do?" The Foundation, based on Paula's ideals of service and compassion, is guided by a vision of a world in which women have achieved social and economic justice. It supports select nonprofits in the San Francisco Bay Area and Chile whose missions are to provide women and girls with reproductive self-determination, healthcare, and education, as well as protection from violence, exploitation, and discrimination.

www.isabelallendefoundation.org
www.isabelallende.com

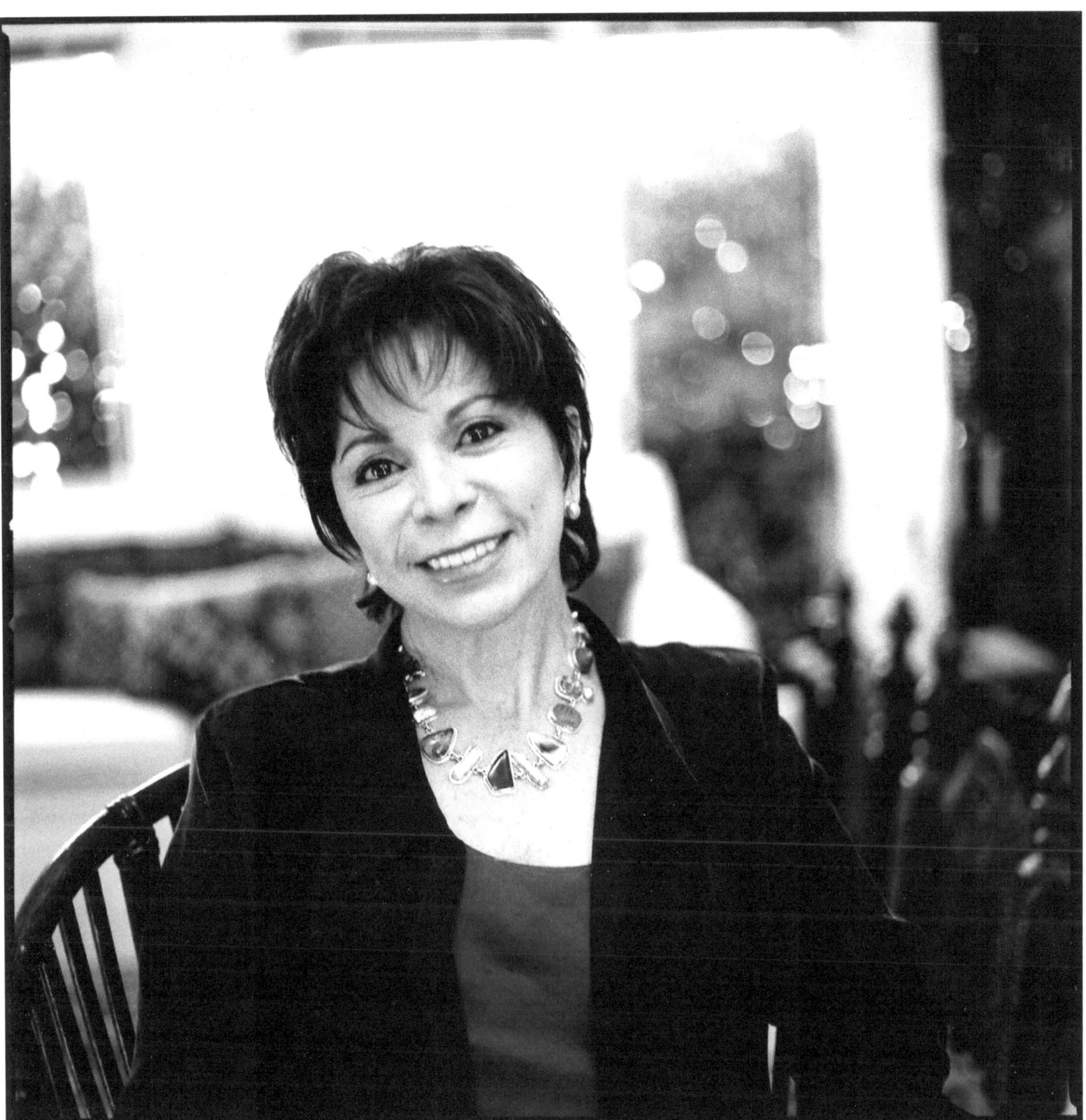

*"My only desire is to have no desires...
pity, that too is a desire."*

LENORE KANDEL
Poet

A student of Zen, colleague of Lawrence Ferlinghetti, Lew Welch and Gary Snyder, and lover/muse to Jack Kerouac, her collection of poems *The Love Book* was banned for obscenity in 1967. She referred to her verse as "holy erotica". Lenore Kandel is considered one of the major poets of the 20th century.

"I left my poems on Lawrence Ferlinghetti's s desk at City Lights... I had just driven cross-country. Later, I heard my words on a loudspeaker. Someone had picked them off his desk and I'd won a poetry contest. What a welcome."

Although her poems have been published worldwide, the only full book of poetry she published during her lifetime was *Word Alchemy*. She passed away on October 18, 2009.

The posthumously-published *Collected Poems of Lenore Kandel* gathers eighty playful poems written throughout her life. Love and playfulness filled her work. Her poem *Circus* ends with this stanza:

> Observe your brethren. Guard your true love.
>
> These are dark latitudes and the ringmaster has wings.
>
> Let the parade begin.
>
> Love me, love my elephant. Love my tiger.
>
> Love my anything. Get in line.

www.lenorekandel.com

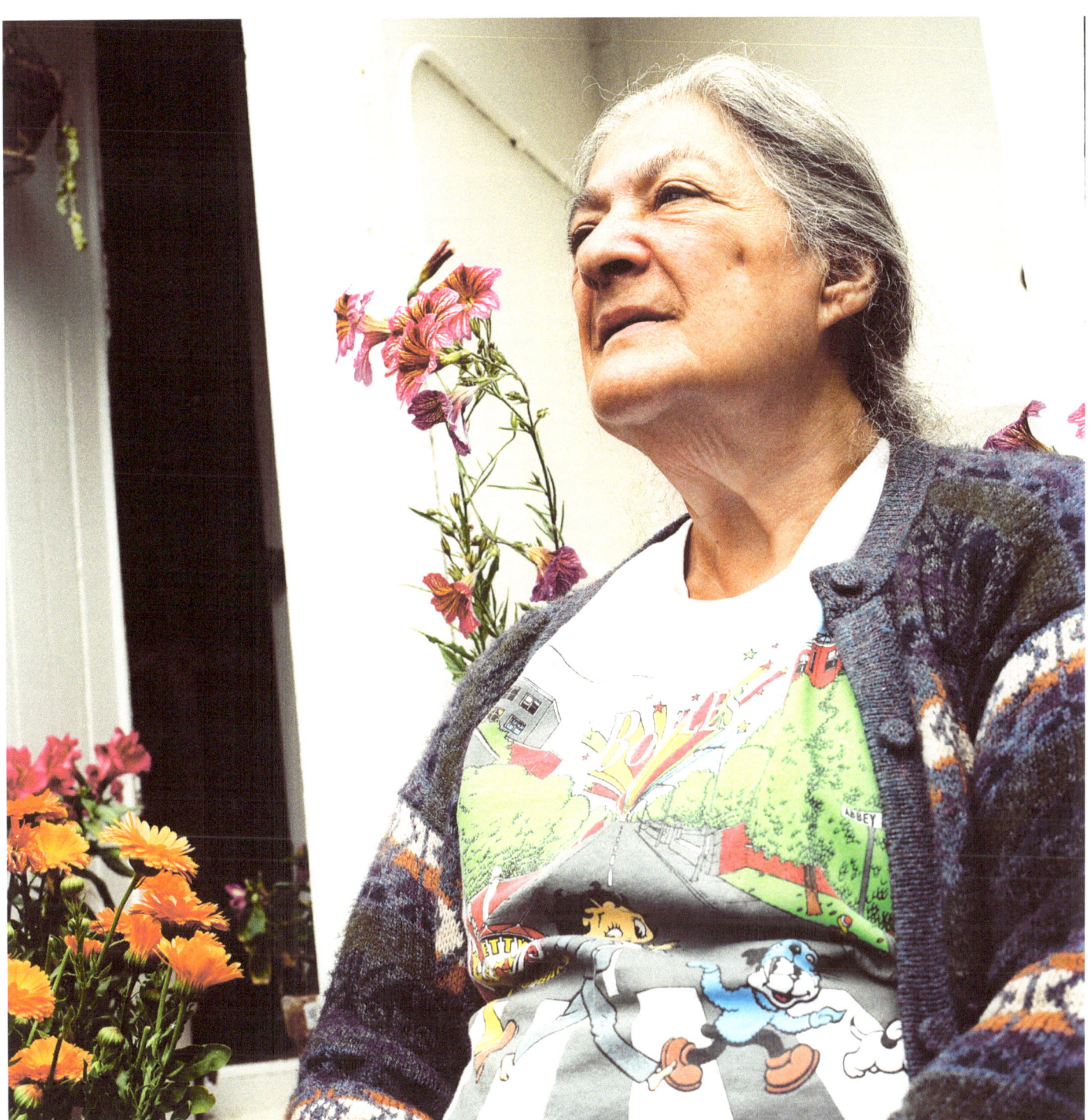

"I've never worried about what audiences would accept or had a game plan regarding career. I never had an idea of how I should look to my fans or anybody else."

ANTONIO BANDERAS
Actor, producer, director

Antonio Banderas has acted in over 70 films, beginning with Almodovar's *Labyrinth of Passion*, breaking into the US industry with *Tie Me Up, Tie Me Down!* A long list of well-known films followed. He's also directed (1999's Crazy in Alabama); and was named World Ambassador of Tourism (with Melanie Griffith) of Spain's Andalucia region, in 2002. Recently he was honored by his native city of Málaga as a "person of good works" and a "universal Malagueño". He's been participating in Holy Week celebrations there since 2011.

Out of the spotlight, the acclaimed actor has long been a supporter of Broadway Cares/Equity Fights AIDS, St. Jude Children's Research Hospital, and UNICEF. Through Green Moon, the production company he created together with his wife, actress Melanie Griffith, he gives young filmmakers a chance.

www.broadwaycares.org
www.stjude.org
www.unicef.org

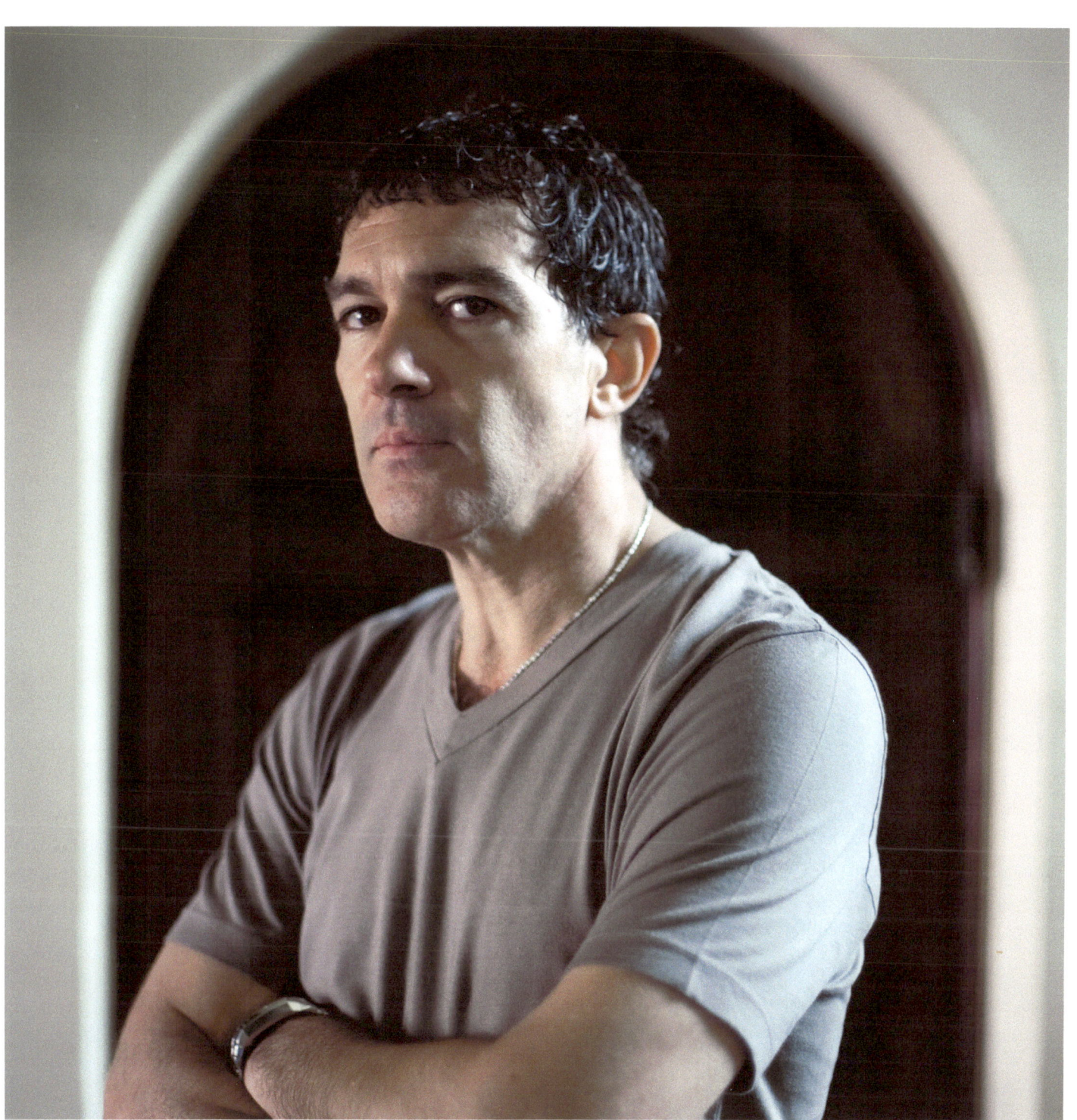

"I'm just a guy who has a need to help show people these situations that are totally forgotten."

JAVIER BARDEM
Actor, documentary producer

Javier Bardem, the winner of a Best Supporting Actor Oscar for his performance in *No Country for Old Men*, wanted to help with the situation in Africa, after having traveled throughout the continent during research for an acting role.

He produced the documentary *Invisibles*, in collaboration with Doctors Without Borders, and recruited five celebrated film directors, including Win Wenders and Isabel Coixet. The film tells five stories about forgotten and unspoken crises: Chagas Disease, sleeping sickness, boy soldiers in Uganda, sexual violence against civilians in the Congo, and displaced people in rural Colombia.

After completing the film, he started working with John Prendergast of the Enough Project, a human rights organization that fights to end genocide and crimes against humanity. This organization started a campaign to Raise Hope for Congo, to protect women in that Central African country.

He went on to produce *Sons of the Clouds: The Last Colony,* a documentary about the Saharawies and their plight to end the invasion of their land by Morocco. Beyond being a multi-generational actor who honors his family with his finely honed his craft, Javier Bardem is secretly a journalist, revealing truths.

www.doctorswithoutborders.org
www.enoughproject.org
www.raisehopeforcongo.org

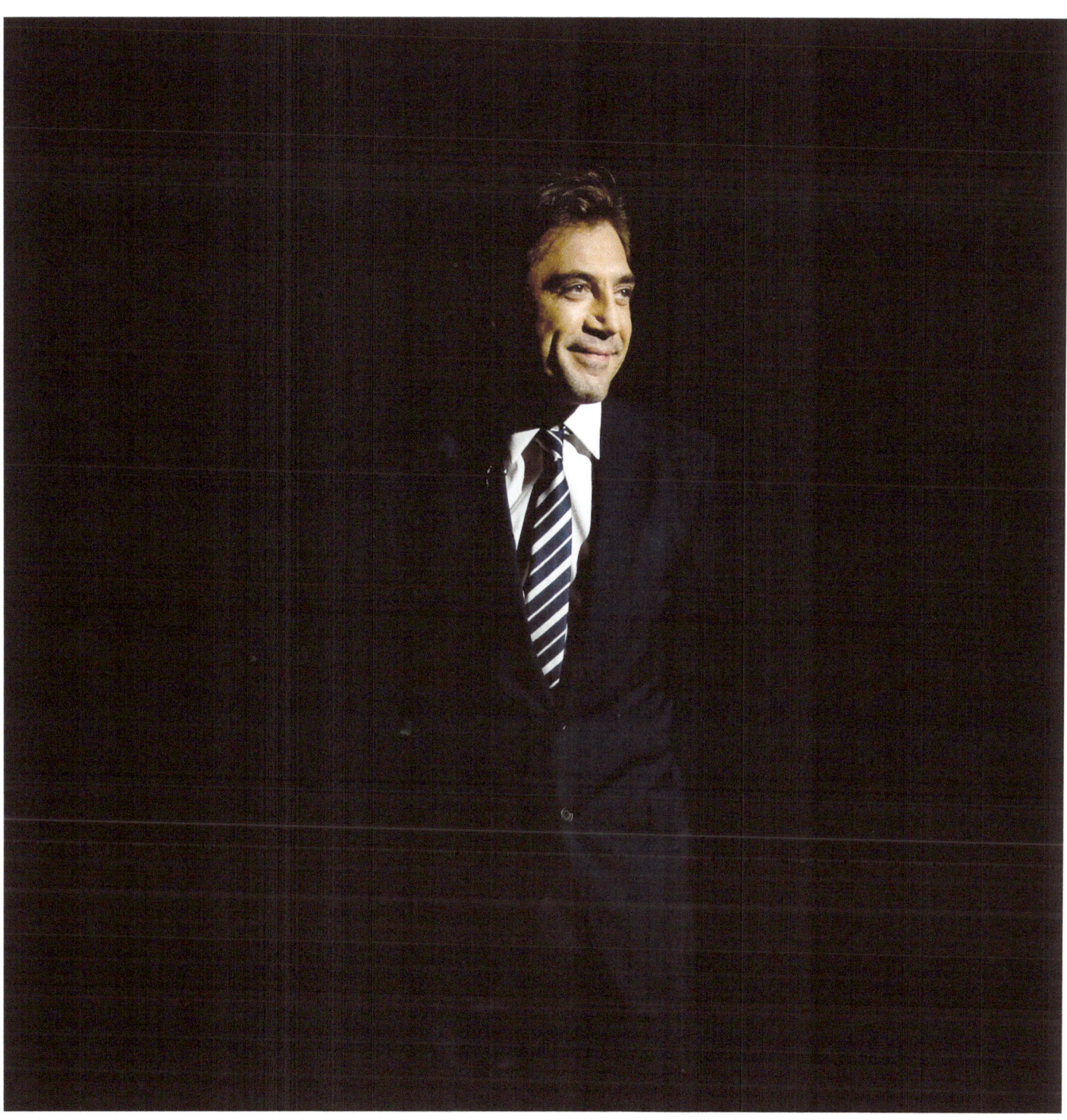

"I don't know what my calling is, but I want to be here for a bigger reason. I strive to be like the greatest people who have ever lived."

WILL SMITH
Actor, director, producer, co-founder of Will and Jada Smith Foundation

Will Smith hosted the Nelson Mandela AIDS benefit concert in George, South Africa, and participated in the *America: A Tribute to Heroes* charity telethon for victims of 9/11, among his frequent non-profit event participation.

The Will and Jada Smith Foundation, formed as a family foundation with wife Jada Pinkett Smith, is "dedicated to the betterment of the world around us," and focuses on education, empowerment, health, community development, sustainability, and the arts. The Foundation donated $1.3 million last year, to a variety of religious, civic and arts groups, including the Youth Health Empowerment Project in Philadelphia (where Will Smith was born and raised), the Lupus Foundation, the Baltimore School for the Arts and the Make-A-Wish Foundation, as well as PACT, which supports special needs children in Baltimore. The couple gave $1 million to help set up a school for children of all religions. They're on the "Giving Back 30" list, of most generous celebrities.

"About ten years ago Jada and I started dreaming about the possibility of creating an ideal educational environment, where children could feel happy, positive and excited about learning," says Smith.

www.wjsff.org
www.y-hep.org
www.pact.kennedykrieger.org

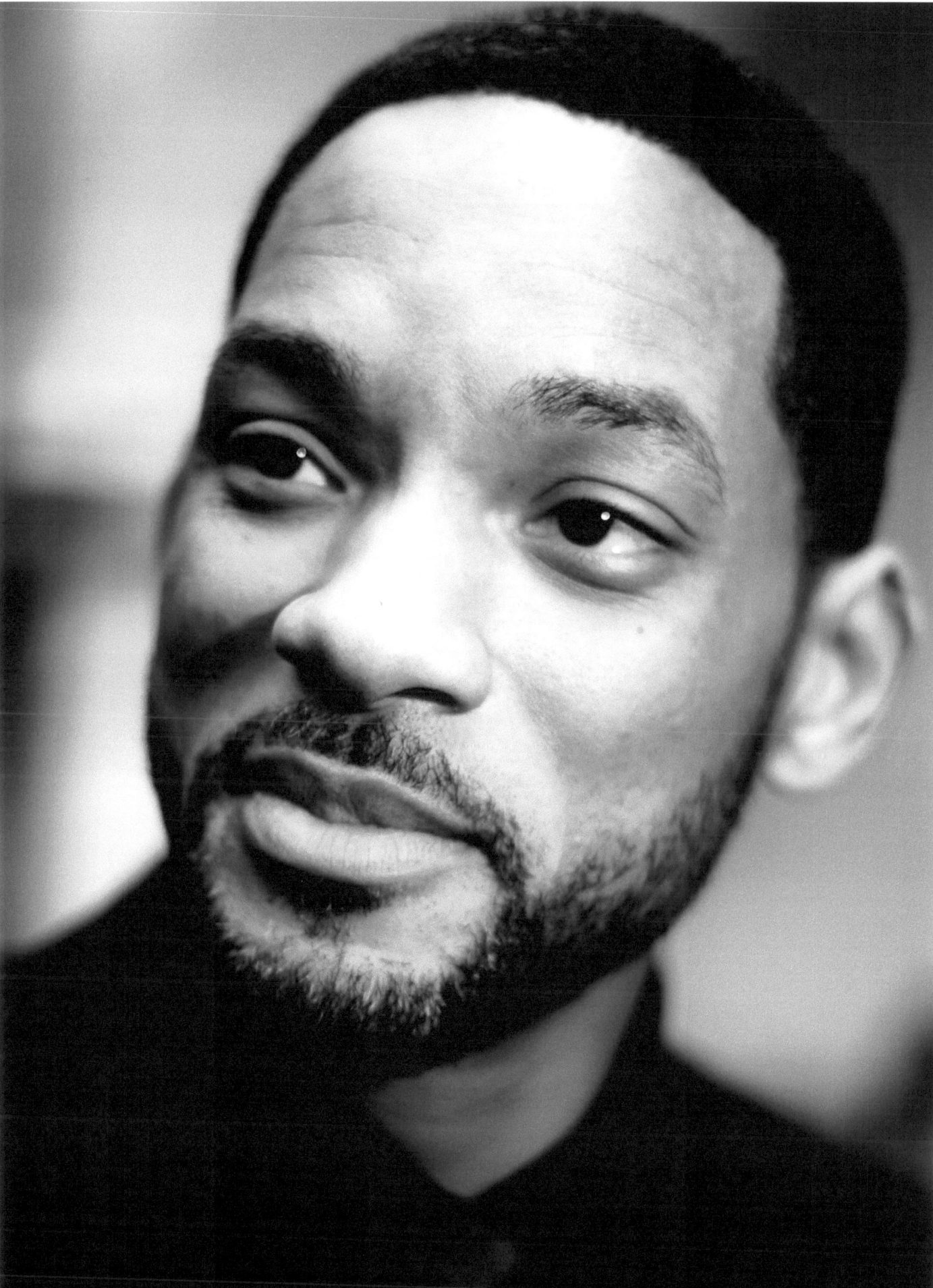

*"Just where you are
Is the nicest place to be.
Just where you are
Earth touches eternity.
Just where you are
The sun shines on the tree.
And where you are
Is never far
From me."*

RAMÓN SENDER BARAYÓN
Composer, writer

Ramón Sender was a key character in the greater Bay Area counterculture, as an electronic music pioneer, co-producer with Steward Brand of the Trips Festival in San Francisco, and co-founder with Limeliter Lou Gottlieb of the open-land Morning Star commune ("The Digger Farm") that morphed into four more Sonoma County intentional communities (both in 1966). In 1962 he co-founded the San Francisco Tape Music Center together with Morton Subotnick, with whom he would develop a voltage-controlled synthesizer. They placed an ad in the paper looking for someone to build their idea, and found Donald Buchla in 1964. This collaboration produced the Buchla Modular Electronic Music System (pictured). One of his most popular pieces of music is Desert Ambulance, whose first performance in 1964 was recorded then and later published by Locust Music on vinyl.

Sender´s books include *A Planetary Sojourn: Stories, Articles, Essays, Letters & Four Recipes for Bliss, Zero Weather,* and *Death in Zamora*, in which he documents the assassination of his mother Amparo Barayón by the forces of Francisco Franco, for refusing to denounce her husband, exiled Spanish Republican writer Ramón J. Sender. Most recently, he wrote a reality fiction novel based on San Francisco Tape Music Center, *Naked Close-Up*.

With his wife, Judith Levy-Sender, he produces in San Francisco a free admission speaker series titled "Odd Mondays," now in its 12th year. Sender supports The Open Land archives, The Great Freedom/Balanced View movement and The Abraham Lincoln Brigade Archives.

www.badabamama.com
www.greatfreedom.org
www.alba-valb.org
www.raysender.com
www.oddmondays.com

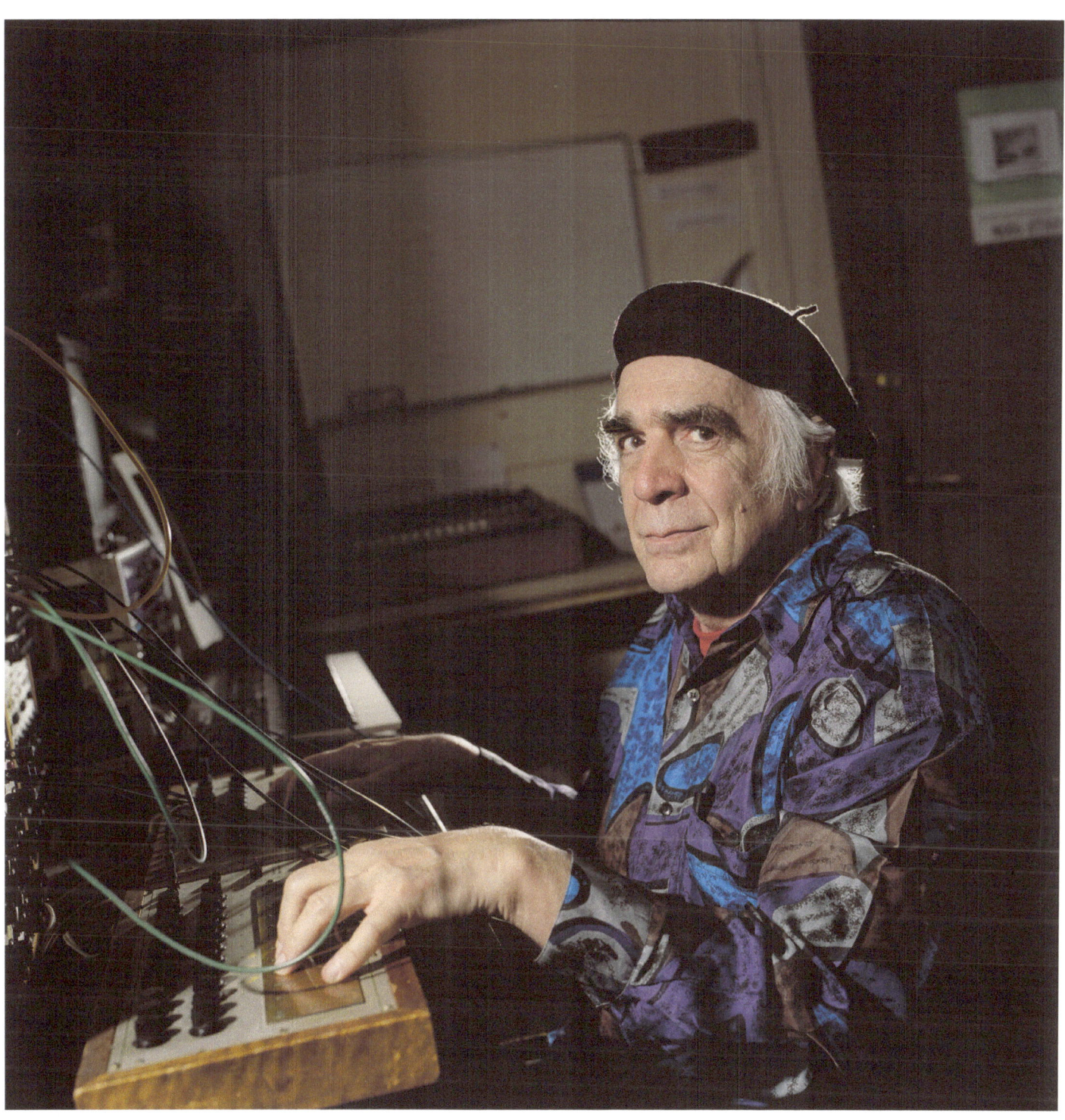

"Despite all of the ghastliness in the world, human beings are made for goodness. The ones that are held in high regard are not militarily powerful, nor even economically prosperous. They have a commitment to try and make the world a better place."

ARCHBISHOP DESMOND TUTU
Archbishop Emeritus of Cape Town, Nobel Peace Laureate, Chair of The Elders

Archbishop Tutu is a veteran anti-apartheid activist and peace campaigner widely regarded as "South Africa's moral conscience". He's one of The Elders, an independent group of global leaders brought together by Nelson Mandela in 2007. They work together to promote peace building, and assist in tackling the causes of human suffering.

Archbishop Tutu spreads hope, love and joy, even in the face of the global challenges he's enthusiastically working to overcome.

www.theelders.org

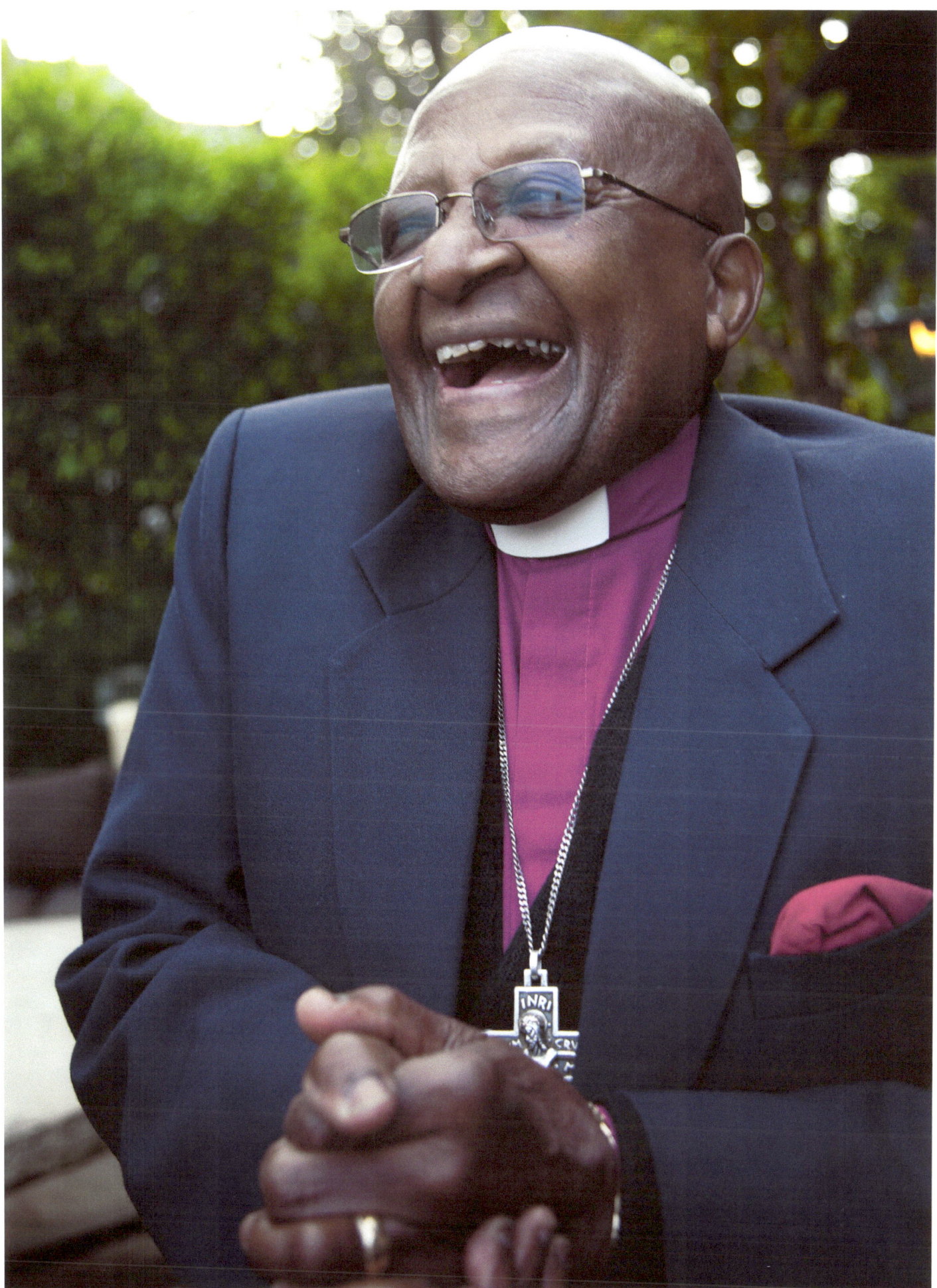

"There is no other organ quite like the uterus. If men had such an organ they would brag about it. So should we."

— Ina May Gaskin

INA MAY GASKIN AND STEPHEN GASKIN
Midwife, writer; founders of The Farm

Ina May and Stephen Gaskin have been champions for natural childbirth, alternative lifestyles, sustainable communities, and organic farming for decades. Ina May developed the Gaskin Maneuver, which uses simple body movements to facilitate a difficult birth. She is the author of *Spiritual Midwifery* and *Ina May's Guide to Childbirth*, and started The Safe Motherhood Quilt Project, a national effort to honor those women who have died of pregnancy-related causes, and to draw public attention to the unchanging maternal death rate in the United States.

Stephen, a veteran of the Korean War, was a teacher at the University of San Francisco when in 1969 the American Academy of Religion sent him on a two-year speaking tour throughout the United States. The caravan grew to 69 buses. In 1971, the group of 1,200 people ended up in Summertown, Tennessee, where they collectively bought land and formed the oldest alternative community in the United States, "The Farm".

Together they helped formed Plenty International, a non-profit organization that assists people in all parts of the world, with the idea that there's plenty for everybody. They also support Farms Not Arms. Both Ina May and Stephen have received the Right Livelihood Award, an alternative to the Nobel. Stephen passed away July 1st, 2014 at the age of 79.

www.thefarm.org
www.plenty.org
www.farmsnotarms.org
www.inamay.com
www.stephengaskin.com

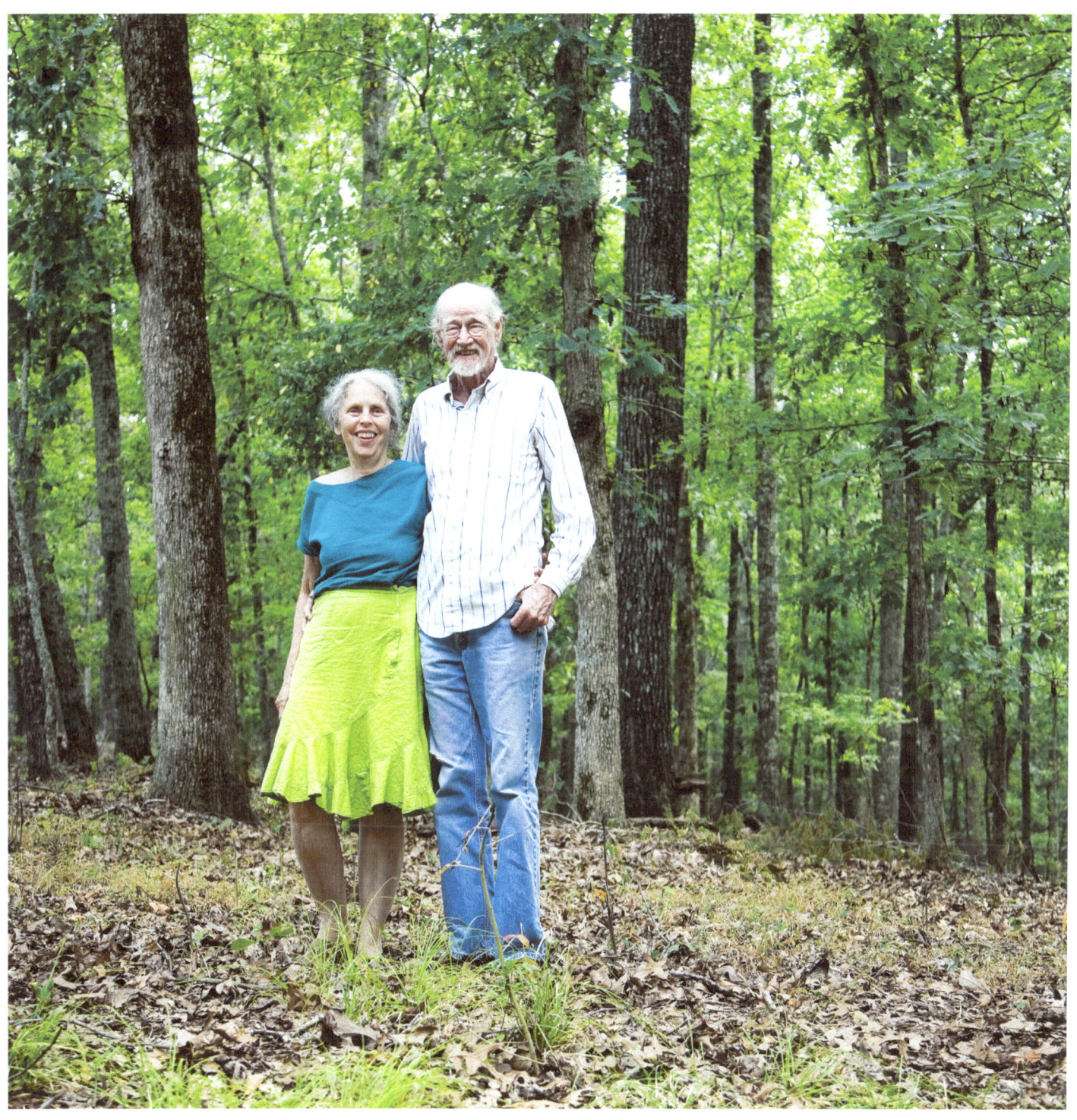

"Music is expression of harmony in sound.
Love is the expression of harmony in life."

— Stephen Gaskin

"Have the courage to dream and dream big! How else can your dreams come true? Live in possibility and take care of your beloved community."

JODIE EVANS

Community, social, political organizer and trouble maker, co-founder of CODEPINK

Jodie Evans co-founded CODEPINK, Women For Peace, a women-initiated grassroots peace and social justice movement working to "end the wars in Iraq and Afghanistan, stop new wars, and redirect our resources into healthcare, education, green jobs and other life-affirming activities, with an emphasis on joy and humor."

Evans serves on the boards of Women's Media Center and Sisterhood is Global Institute. "At SIGI we are developing a platform to help organize, democratize and increase the volume of the Global Women's Movement. This is needed to make war obsolete."

She also co-founded 826LA with writer Dave Eggers, an after-school writing program in Venice, California. She serves on the boards of 826LA, Rainforest Action Network, Drug Policy Alliance and the Institute for Policy Studies.

www.codepink4peace.org
www.sigi.org
www.ran.org
www.826la.org
www.drugpolicy.org
www.ips-dc.org

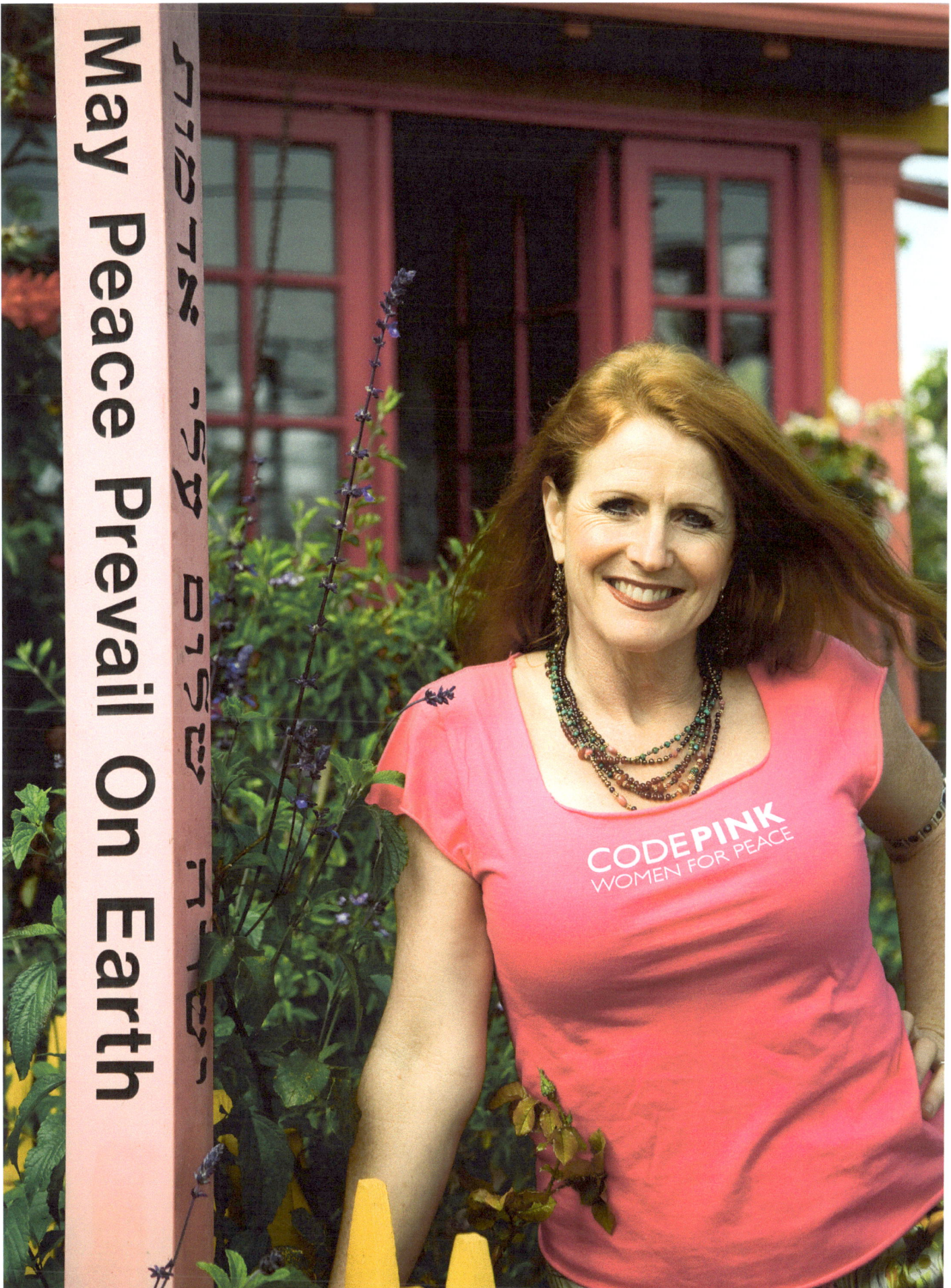

"Trickster narration is a useful hermeneutics for transcending the oversimplified binary thinking so prevalent in Western thought ... humans must constantly be wary, because Raven is always hiding in the shadows. It is human to make mistakes. But how do we collectively learn from those mistakes?"

— From *Ravens, Storms, and the Ecological Indian at the National Museum of the American Indian,* Wicaso Sa Review, 21

MELISSA K. NELSON
Cultural ecologist, professor

Melissa Nelson, Ph.D., serves as president of The Cultural Conservancy, and associate professor of American Indian Studies at San Francisco State University. The Cultural Conservancy, an indigenous rights nonprofit organization, is dedicated to the preservation and revitalization of indigenous cultures and their ancestral lands.

In 2005, Melissa co-produced an award-winning documentary film, *The Salt Song Trail: Bringing Creation Back Together.* Her first book, *Original Instructions: Indigenous Teachings for a Sustainable Future*, an edited anthology of over twenty indigenous leaders, was published in 2008.

Melissa is an enrolled member of the Turtle Mountain Band of Chippewa Indians of North Dakota and is of mixed-blood heritage: Chippewa (Anishinaabe) and French-Cree (Métis) from her mother, and Norwegian from her father, born and raised in northern California.

www.earthdiver.org

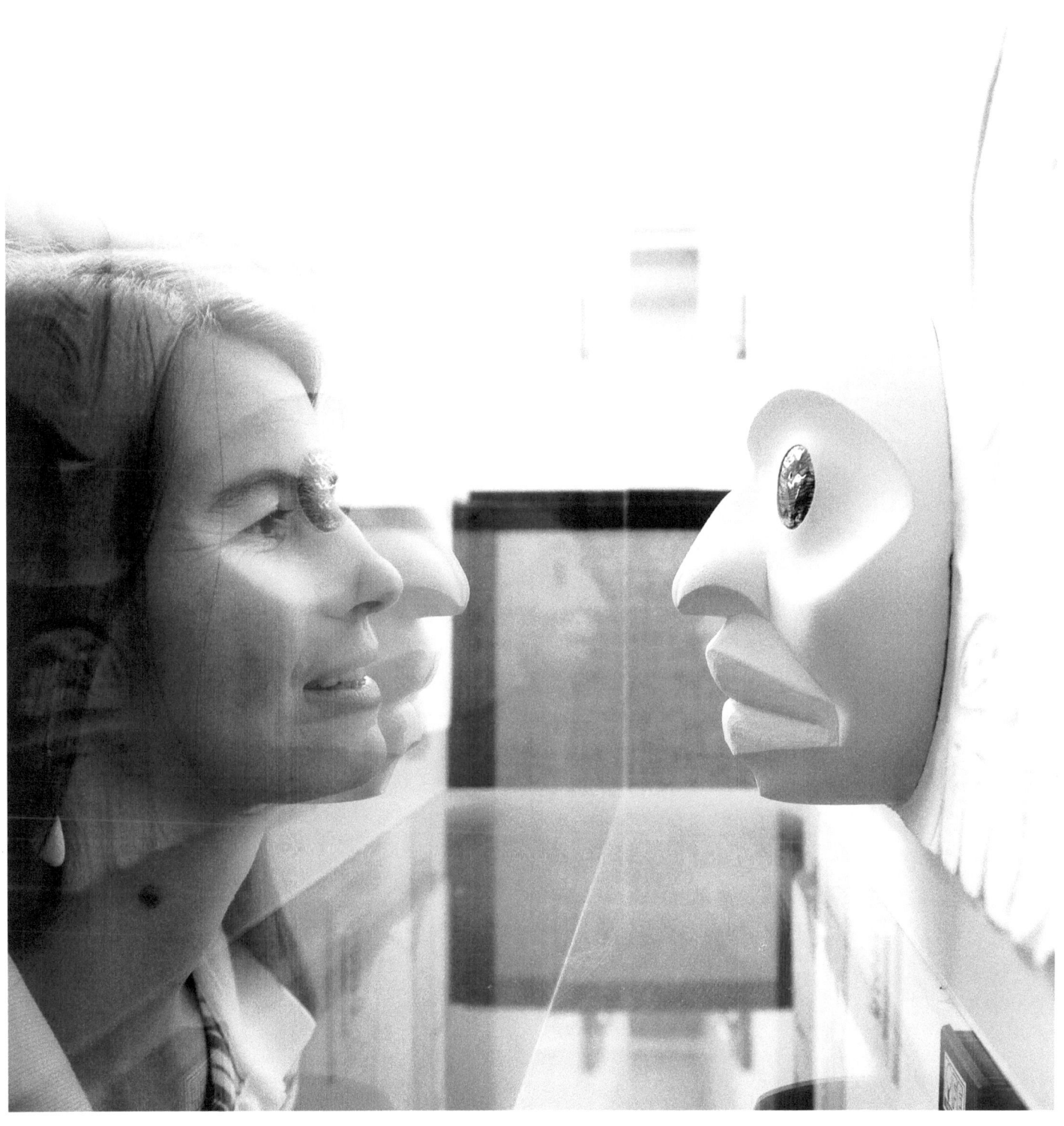

"Being for life has no arbitrary limit, and our need to learn humility as a species in the cosmos may be directly connected with the mundane atrocities we struggle against daily."

MICHAEL ROSSMAN
Key leader of the Free Speech Movement, professor, author

In December 1964, the UC Berkeley faculty voted to support demands by the Free Speech Movement, in which Rossman was one of the student leaders, that the university not be allowed to regulate speech. The Free Speech Movement "is generally regarded as the progenitor of anti-war and civil rights protests and student movements in general that swept American campuses over the next decades", according to the San Francisco Chronicle in Rossman's obituary. He died on May 12, 2008.

Michael Rossman wrote a critical analysis of the learning process and a more creative, self-guided, intuitive approach to education, *On Learning and Social Change* (available for free on his website). And starting in 1977, Rossman collected 25,000 social and political progressive movement posters in the All of Us or None archive. The collection is now part of the Oakland Museum of California.

Rossman dedicated his time to social justice and environmental education for children, as an elementary science teacher, first at the Berkeley Montessori School, then at Ecole Bilingue in Emeryville, California. He also helped run Camp Chrysalis, a summer program that took children to state parks around Northern California, for 25 years.

www.mrossman.org

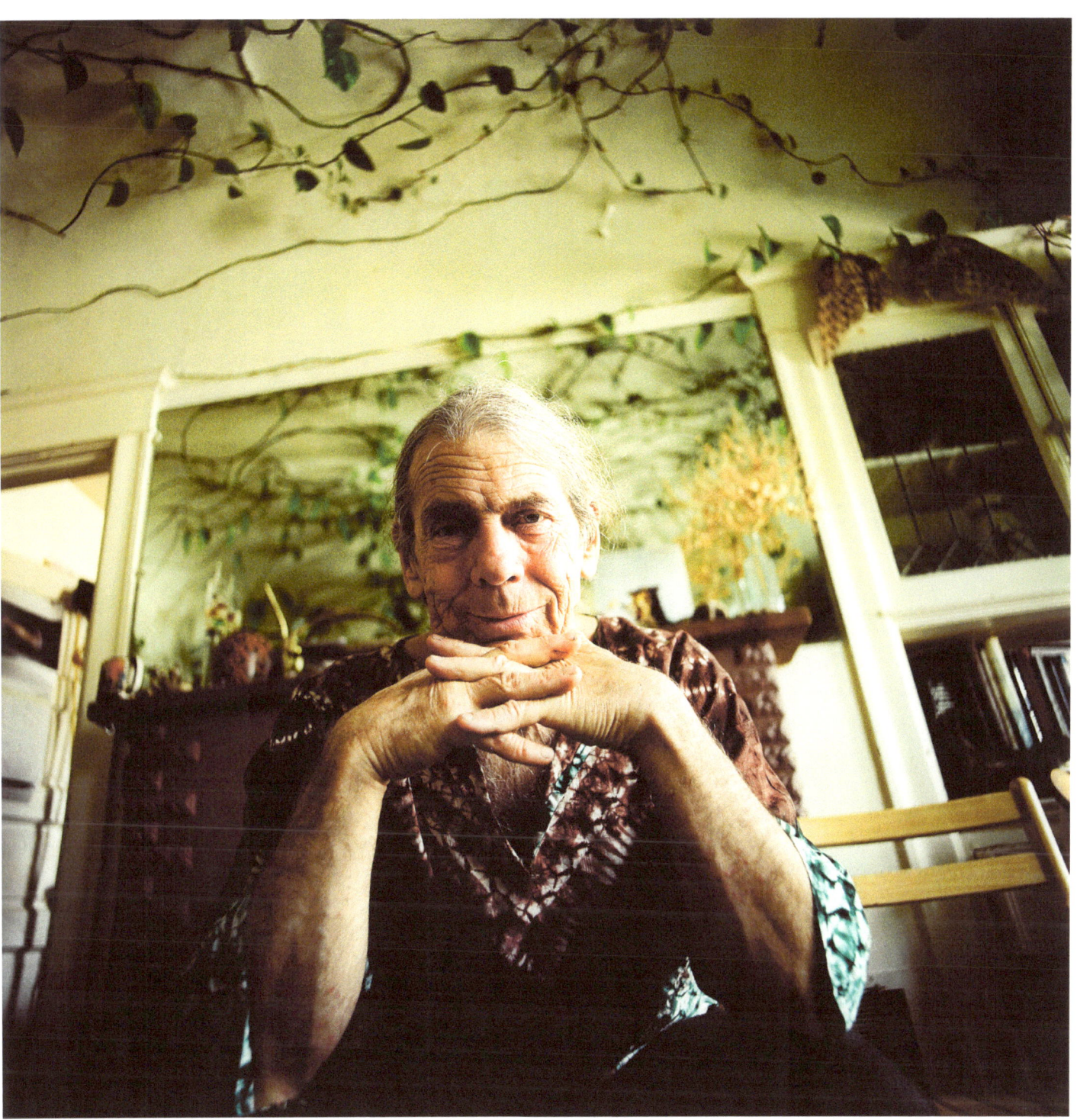

"Be serious about your passions, but NEVER take yourself seriously!"

NANCY KOPPELMAN
Global Citizen

Nancy has been committed to women's rights and health issues since working in the women's health care movement in the early 70's. Together with Connie Smith and Sandra Tyler, Nancy Koppelman co-founded the Global Neighborhood Fund, a giving circle to provide grants to social justice causes around the world, focusing first in Liberia.

Since 2001 she's been involved with Direct Relief International, a global medical and disaster relief organization. She created Women for Direct Relief, and curely serves on the board of directors.

In 2007, Nancy became a member of President Obama's National Finance Committee, and continues to serve with the Democratic National Committee.

She's also an ambassador for UCSB Arts and Lectures, hosting many artists and activists at her home. She's on the advisory board of the Aspen Brain Forum, and is a Fellow at the Aspen Institute. She has served on the Harvard women's leadership board, and with Human Rights Watch Santa Barbara.

An avid traveler, Nancy has been to over 50 countries around the globe. She and her husband Larry split their time between Santa Barbara, California, and Aspen, Colorado.

www.globalneighborhoodfund.org
www.directrelief.org
www.artsandlectures.sa.ucsb.edu
www.aspenbrainforum.com
www.aspeninstitute.org

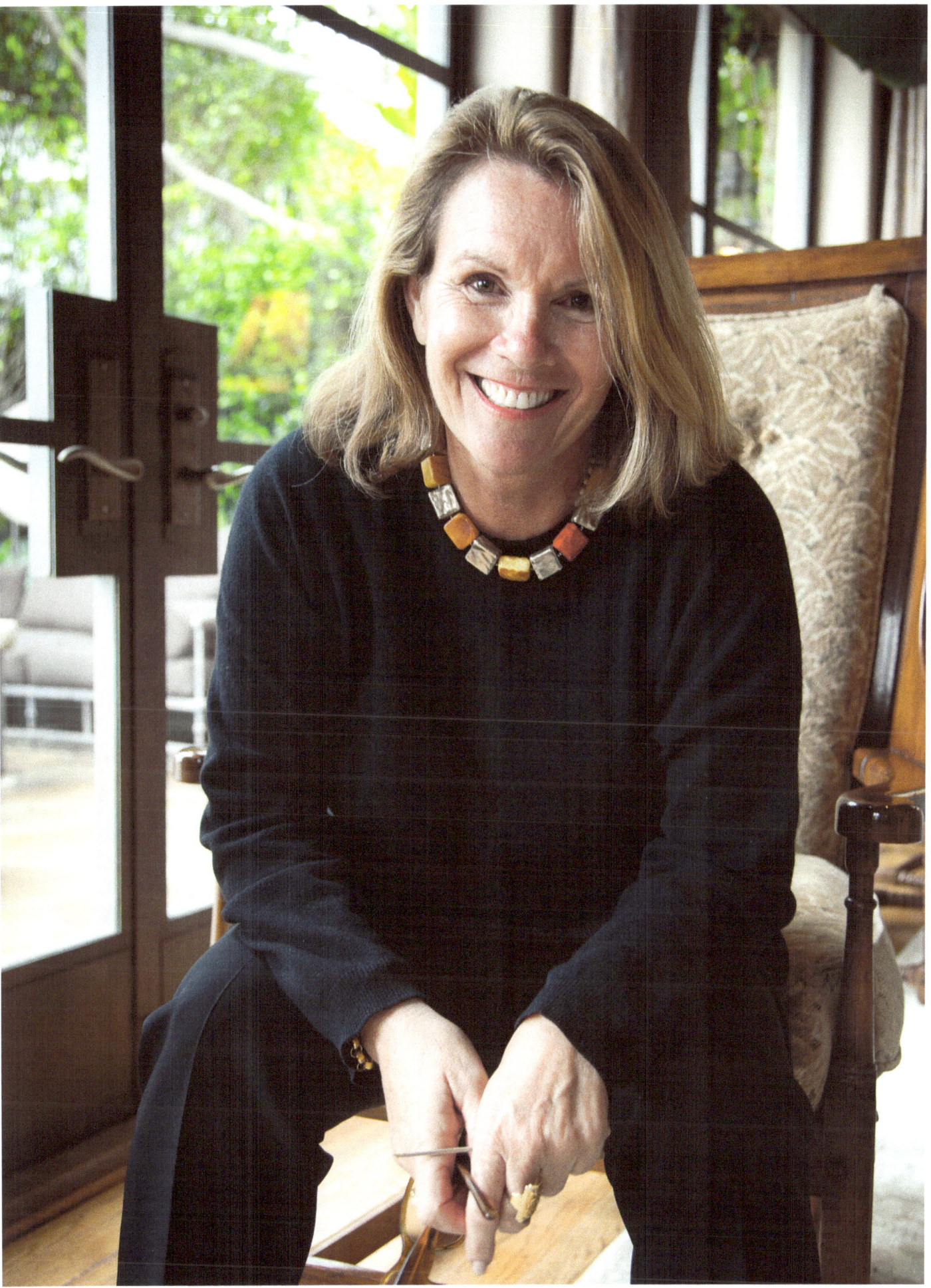

"Gardening is something that connects all of us. The process is nurturing. When you see the lives of many mentally ill people or people on the outs, you find out there have been very few opportunities to be nurtured or to nurture. In the simplicity there's an opportunity for reflection, and an opportunity for respite, to get out of your head; that's part of the therapy."

OSCAR CARMONA
Founder, Healing Grounds Nursery

Oscar Carmona has been inspiring others with urban gardens for over 25 years, living by the motto, "Feed the soil and let the plants feed you." Carmona was raised in the city, five miles from downtown Los Angeles, where at a young age he started to play in the dirt with his first garden. During his later travels in South America in 1982, Carmona discovered the fundamental connection between seeds and people.

Graduating with a degree in Fine Art from the University of California Santa Barbara in 1983, Oscar fell in love with farming, and has been using his creative energy towards the art of growing plants. In 1986, he started a horticultural therapy program at the Alpha Resource Center, working with developmentally challenged adults. Soon after, Carmona became Director of Garden Programs for the Community Environmental Council. From 1991 to 2004, he managed the City of Santa Barbara's community gardens, the CEC's Urban Farm, and began different school gardening programs, as well as a Farming Fun Summer Camp. In 2004, he founded Healing Grounds Nursery to provide work training and income to adults with mental illness through Santa Barbara County Mental Health Services.

Carmona is now deeply involved with the program "Grow Your Own Way / La Comida Crece en Casa", teaching Santa Barbara Food Bank recipients to grow their own food. Carmona's mission is to spread the love for farming and food gardening throughout his community and beyond. He not only teaches at the Santa Barbara Food Bank, but also at Santa Barbara City College and at Santa Maria's Alan Hancock College, both in English and Spanish.

www.healinggroundsnursery.com

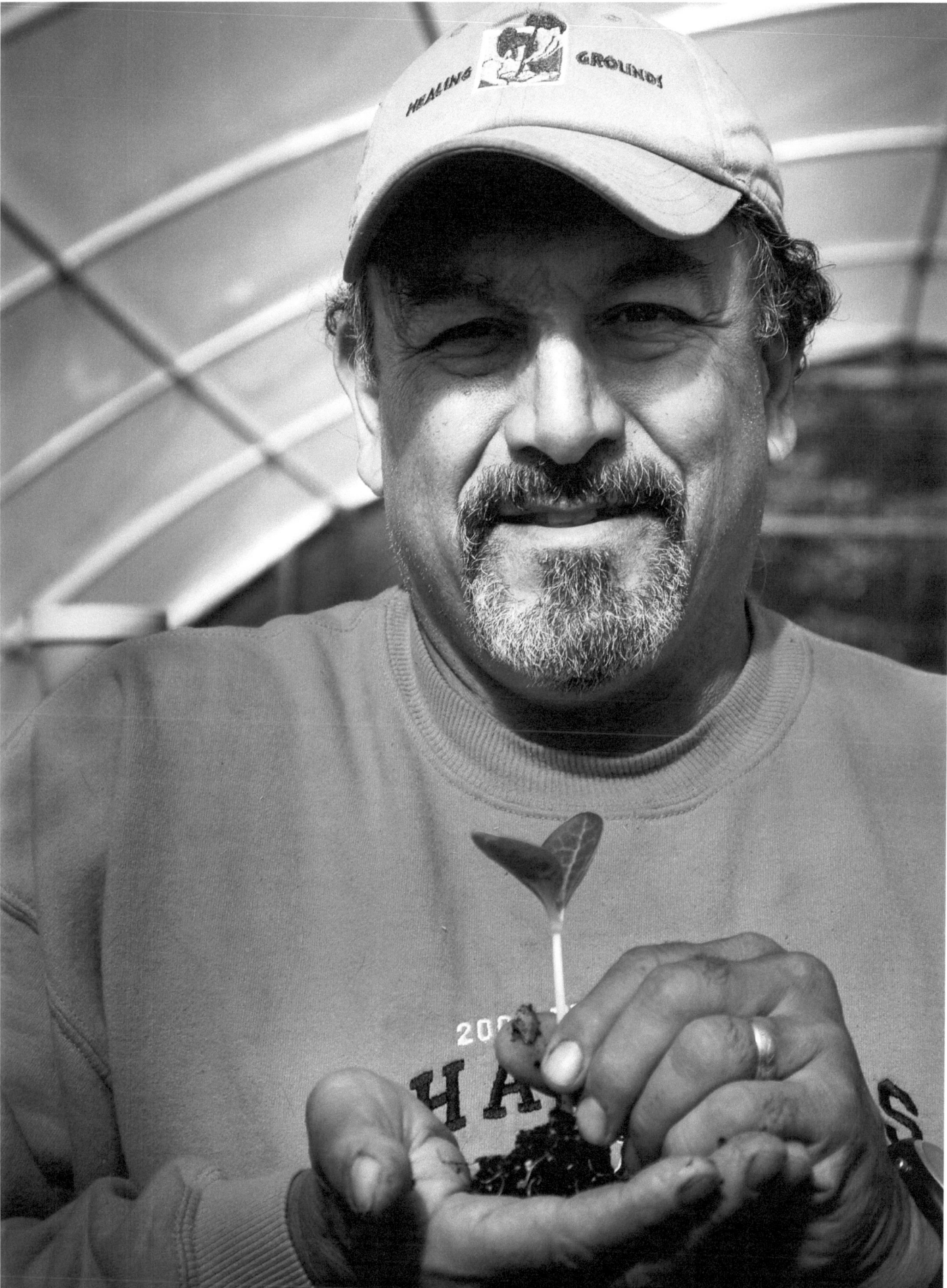

"Every mother counts, and healthcare is a human right."

ROBIN LIM, CPM
Founder, Bumi Sehat Foundation, Indonesia

Every day on earth 981 women, in the prime of their lives, die due to complications of pregnancy or childbirth. Robin Lim is committed to reducing maternal and infant mortality by supporting the midwifery-to-mother-care model throughout the world. FOr her life-saving work, Lim won the CNN Hero of the Year Award in 2011.

In 2005, Lim founded Bumi Sehat Foundation, a non-profit, village-based organization that runs two free community health centers in Bali and Aceh, Indonesia.

In 2011 alone, the clinics provided over 33,000 events of health, education and human services, welcoming over 600 new babies into the world each year. Additionally, Bumi Sehat provides 24-hour emergency services, free and confidential HIV testing, as well as complementary health therapies including acupuncture, cranial sacral therapy, prenatal yoga, elderly yoga, naturopathy, and massage. Bumi Sehat Foundation's educational initiatives include supporting marginalized young women through college to become teachers, nurses or midwives.

The Bumi Sehat Youth Center provides teenagers with computer skills and language courses, as well as capacity building, sex education, recycling and organic gardening. Lim meets with student midwives and nurses from all over Indonesia and The Philippine Islands, to promote natural gentle childbirth and breastfeeding support.

www.bumisehatfoundation.org
www.robinlimsupport.org

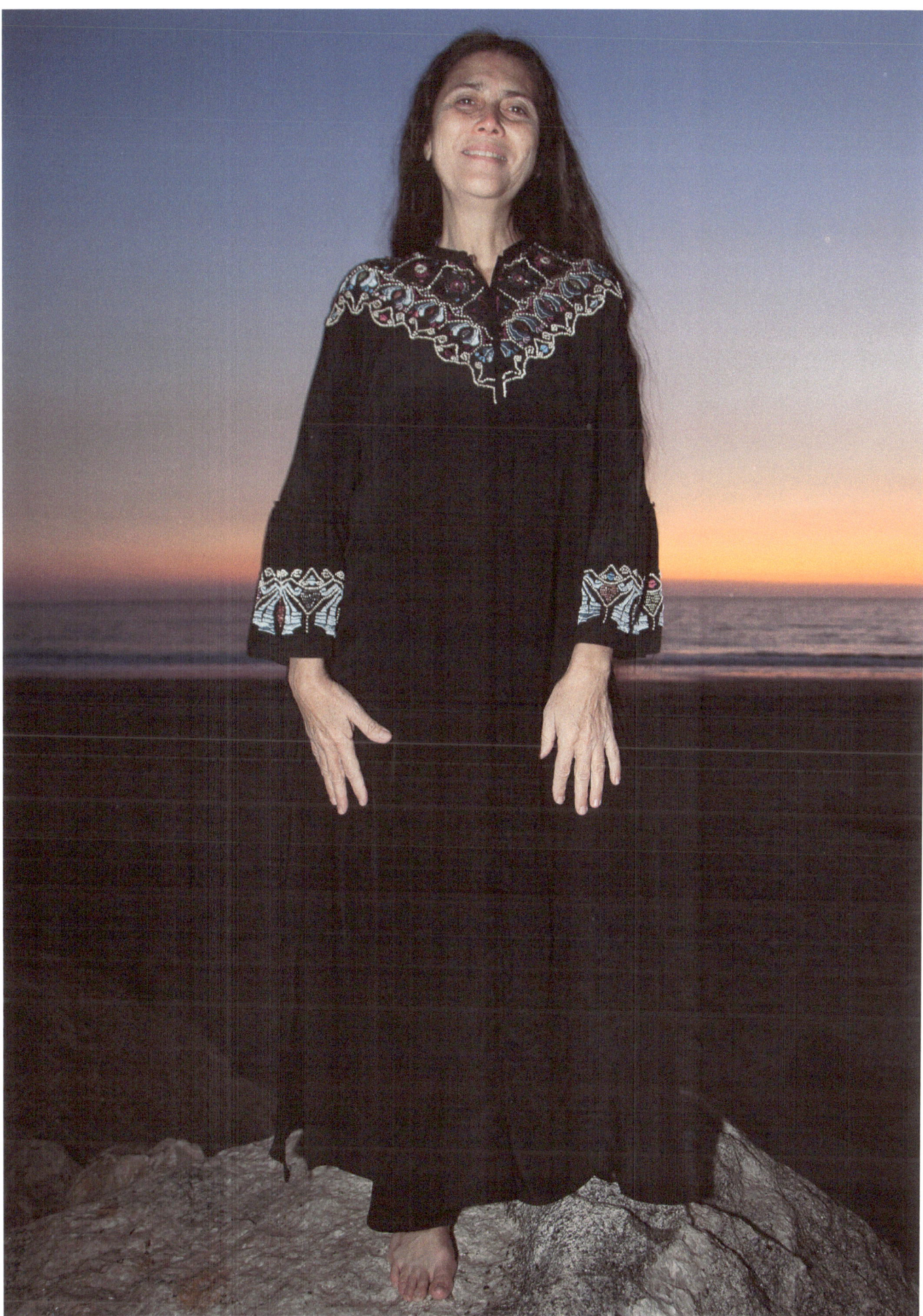

"When you give a child a book, you're giving them a chance for a better future."

VICKI POLLACK
Founder of Children's Book Project

The Children's Book Project distributes free books to children that otherwise wouldn't have books in their homes. Since their beginning in 1992, they have collected and distributed two million books to San Francisco Bay Area children and their shelters, schools, community and daycare centers.

In the sixties, Pollack participated in the civil rights movement, including the Virginia Drug Fair sit-in. Later in San Francisco, she was part of the Diggers, running the free store in the Haight-Ashbury district, which gave away free food and clothing, and cooking for thousands during the Summer of Love.

www.childrensbookproject.org

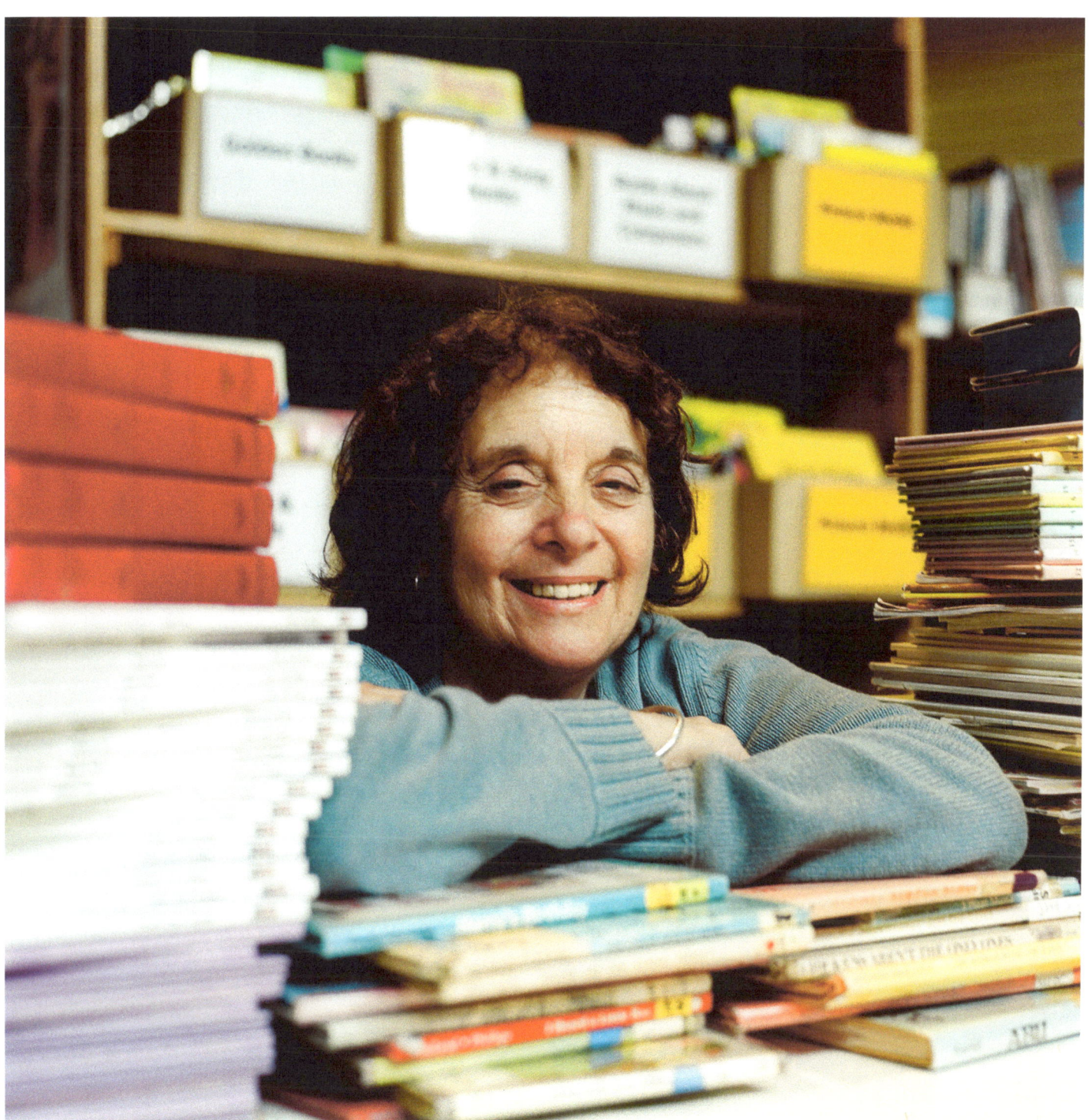

"Back in the ancient times (the sixties), I used to open for a piano player named Thelonius Monk, who once told me, 'Everyone is a genius at just being themselves.' So I try to be the best Wavy Gravy I can muster — always putting my good where it will do the most."

WAVY GRAVY
Clown, co-founder The Seva Foundation, author, artist, co-director Camp Winnarainbow

Rock icon Wavy Gravy founded Camp Winnarainbow, a circus summer camp in the Bay Area, that provides scholarships to homeless children and Native American Lakota kids from the Pine Mountain Reservation in South Dakota.

He also co-founded The Seva Foundation, a non-profit organization which alleviates suffering caused by disease and poverty worldwide, and is committed to health, cultural survival and sustainable communities.

Wavy, known as "the MC of Woodstock" and probably the world's most beloved rock and roll clown, also entertains kids at the Children's Cancer Research Institute in San Francisco. He wrote the children's book *Something Good for a Change*, about a boy who loses his hair due to chemotherapy.

www.seva.org
www.campwinnarainbow.org

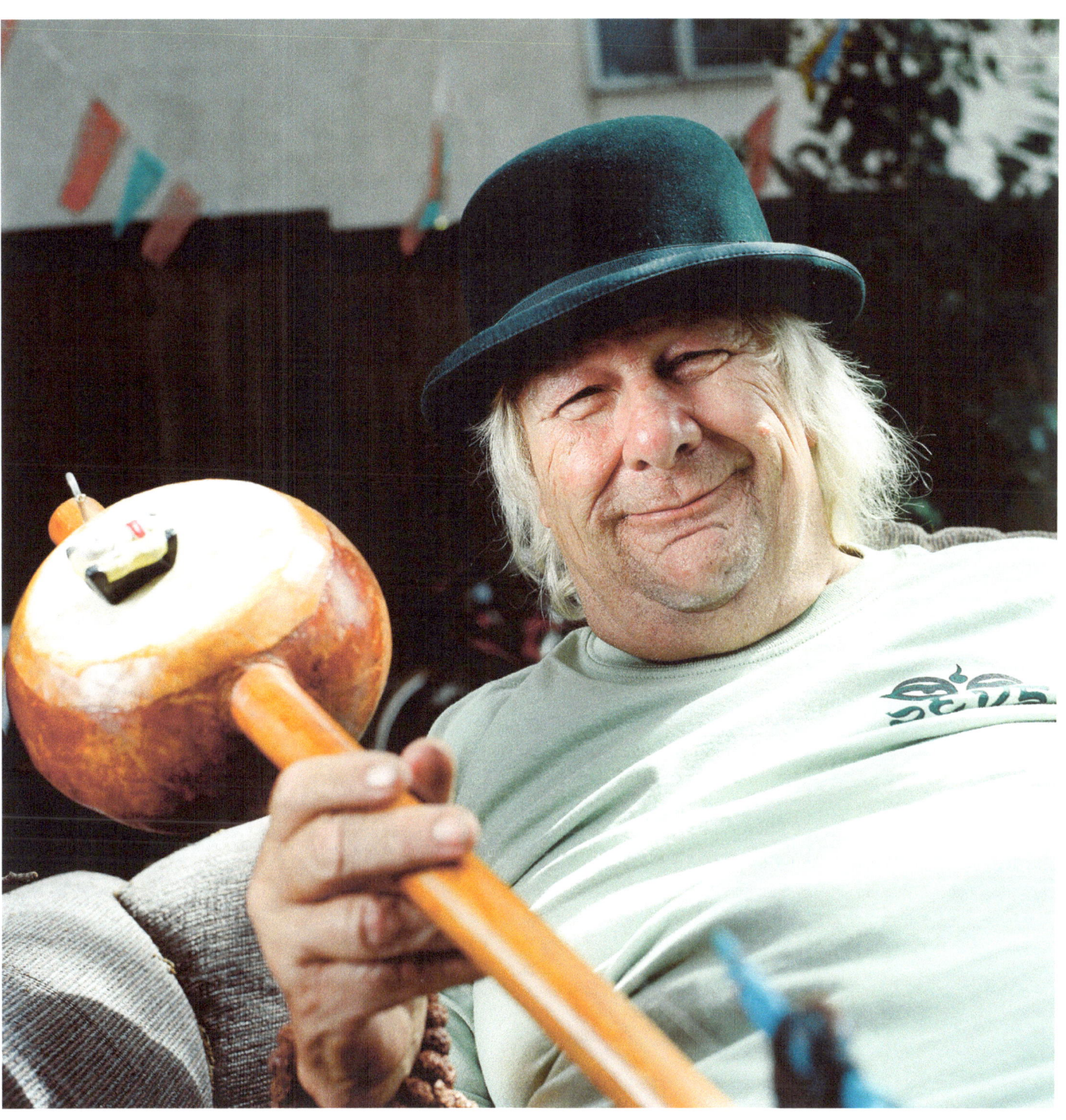

"War is not a computer-generated missile striking a digital map. War is the color of earth as it explodes in our faces, the sound of a child pleading, the smell of smoke and fear. Women survivors of war are not the single image portrayed on the television screen, but the glue that holds families and countries together. Perhaps by understanding women, and the other side of war... we will have more humility in our discussions of wars... perhaps it is time to listen to women's side of history."

— From *The Other Side of War*

ZAINAB SALBI
Co-founder Women for Women International, author

Zainab Salbi wrote a rivetting memoir of her time as the daughter of Saddam Hussein's private pilot: *Between Two Worlds: Escape from Tyranny: Growing Up in the Shadow of Saddam*. She escaped Iraq, and formed Women for Women to help other women whose lives had been torn apart by war. Her most recent book, *If You Knew Me You Would Care*, documents the lives of women refugees of war, illustrated with photographs by Rennio Maifredi. Her previous book, *The Other Side of War: Women's Stories of Survival and Hope*, chronicles the inspiring stories of women who overcame the horrors of war to rebuild their families and countries.

Women for Women provides women survivors of war with an annual program including sponsorship, economic stability, rights awareness, support and safety networks. Women receive a small stipend, with access to market research and entrepreneurial training, cooperative enterprises and post-program microlending, as well as support groups. But most important are the letters from "sister" sponsors in another country. For many women living in war, these letters are a lifeline to peace.

www.womenforwomen.org
www.zainabsalbi.com

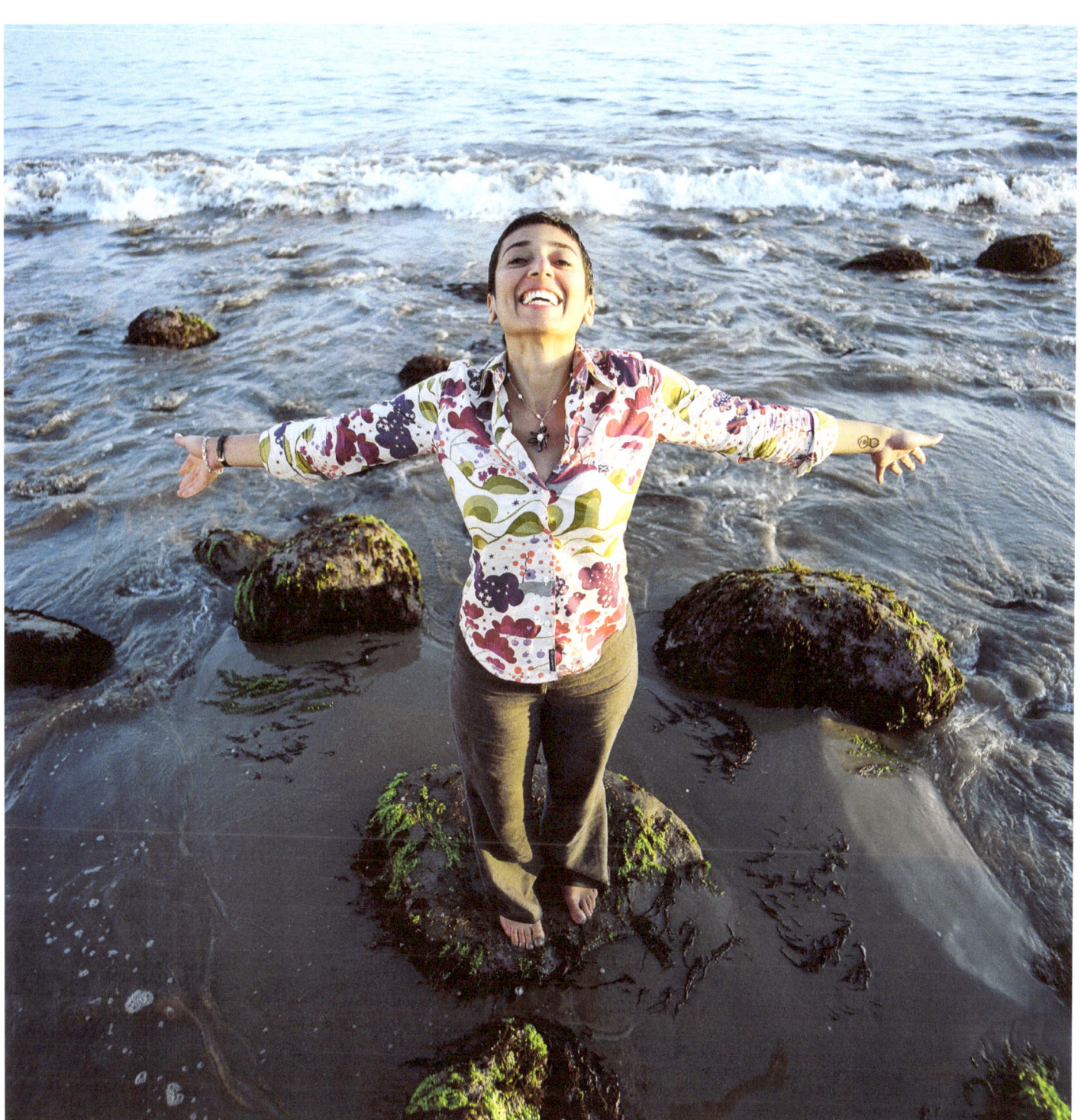

"Sustainability is not a far-off unattainable goal; it's a practical way to solve more than one problem at once."

ANDY LIPKIS
Founder of TreePeople

Andy Lipkis was 15 years old when he began planting trees to rehabilitate smog- and fire-damaged areas in Southern California's mountains. While still in college, he founded TreePeople, and has served as its president since 1973. Since that time, Andy has spearheaded an approach using trees and forest-inspired technologies to make cities sustainable while mitigating floods, drought, pollution, and global warming. These "Functioning Community Forests" are being demonstrated in Los Angeles as a model for cities everywhere.

TreePeople volunteers have planted more than two million trees in the Los Angeles area over the past thirty years. Their work unites the power of trees, people and technology to grow a sustainable future for Los Angeles. From training communities to plant and care for trees, to educating children and adults about the environment, to working with government agencies on critical water issues, TreePeople's work is about helping nature heal our cities.

www.treepeople.org

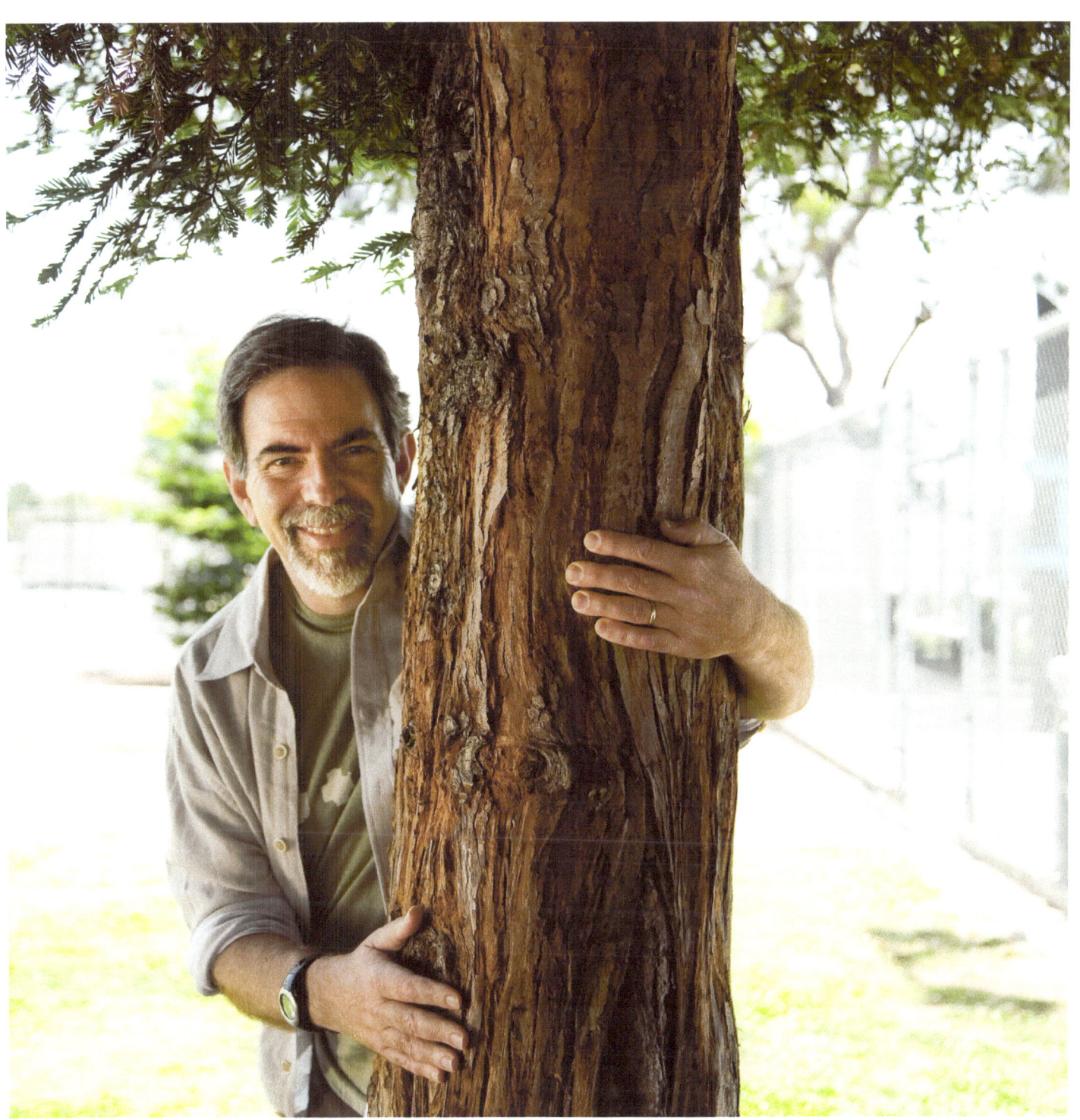

"I have an obligation as an elder to pass on my life experiences to youngsters."

BUD BOTTOMS
Sculptor, co-founder of Get Oil Out

Bud Bottoms, fascinated by creatures from snails to condors, has provided fountains and monuments to Puerta Vallarta, Mexico; Tokyo and Toba City, Japan; Dingle, Ireland; the Shriner's Hospital for Crippled Children in Los Angeles; the Long Beach Aquarium; Monterey Plaza Hotel; Malibu's Michael Landon Park; Oahu, Hawaii; and the beloved landmark dolphin fountain near the wharf in Santa Barbara.

He also co-founded Get Oil Out, a non-profit organization formed after the oil spill of 1969 that despoiled the Santa Barbara coastline. From these beginnings, the modern environmental movement began to form, the California Environmental Quality Act was created (decades later still serving as the strongest environmental law in the world), and Earth Day was born.

www.getoilout.org
www.budbottoms.com

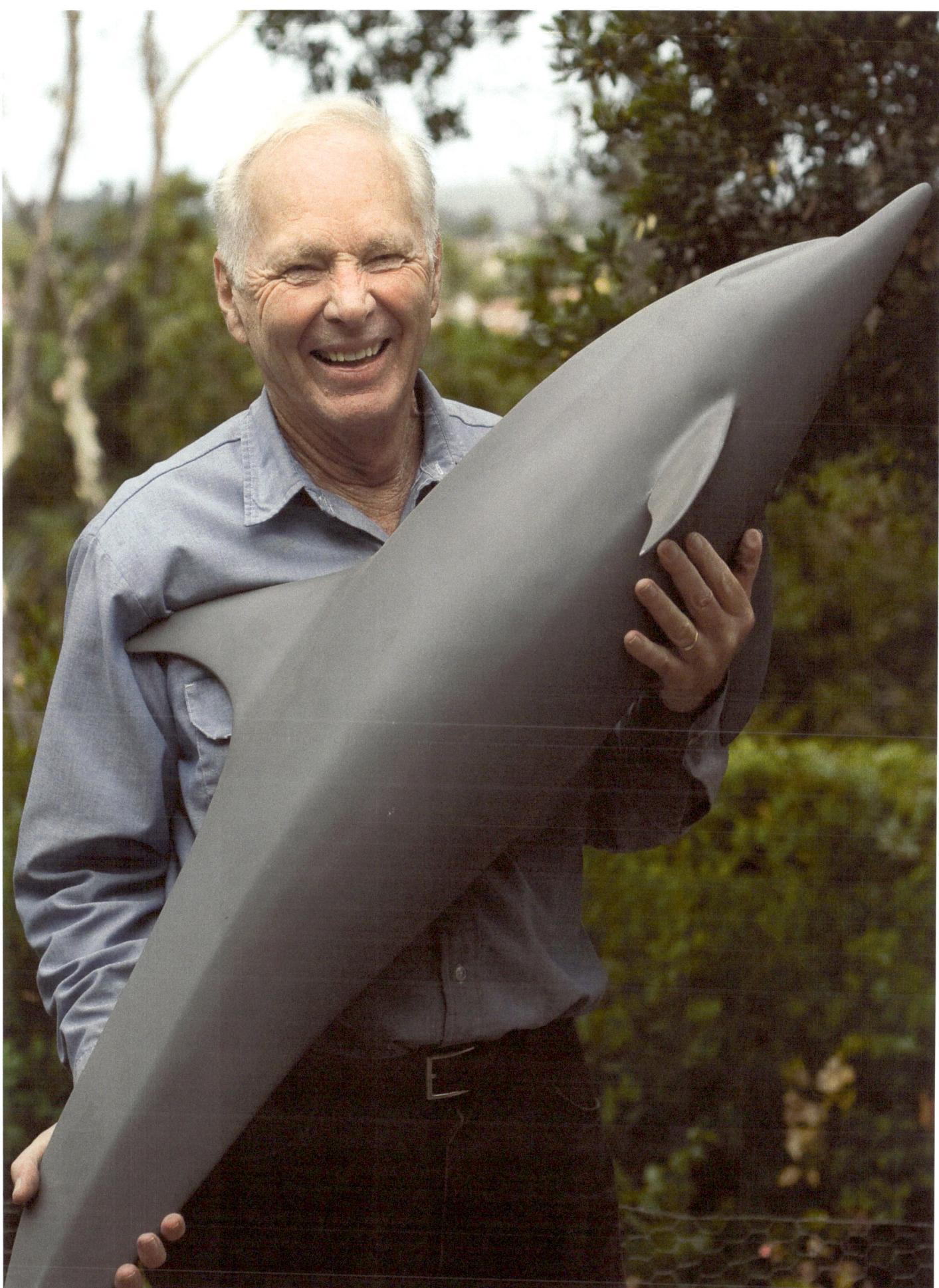

"The best way to predict the future is to create it. Redesigning the future is no longer simply an option but an imperative."

HAROLD POWELL
Environmental designer, builder, sustainable pioneer

Harold Powell studied with Buckminster Fuller and other visionaries in the 70s, bringing the concept of self-sufficient sustainable design and general systems theory to every project he's built. He's worked with nonprofit organizations such as Dwelling Design Network, the Associated Scholars Cooperative, World Game Workshop and Earth Metabolic Design. His homes and work spaces incorporate energy production and efficiencies, smart water use, organic food production and use innovative regenerative resources. As head of design for Helical Systems, Powell is developing fully integrated sustainable communities utilizing state of the art modular housing systems.

www.teliosenvironmental.com

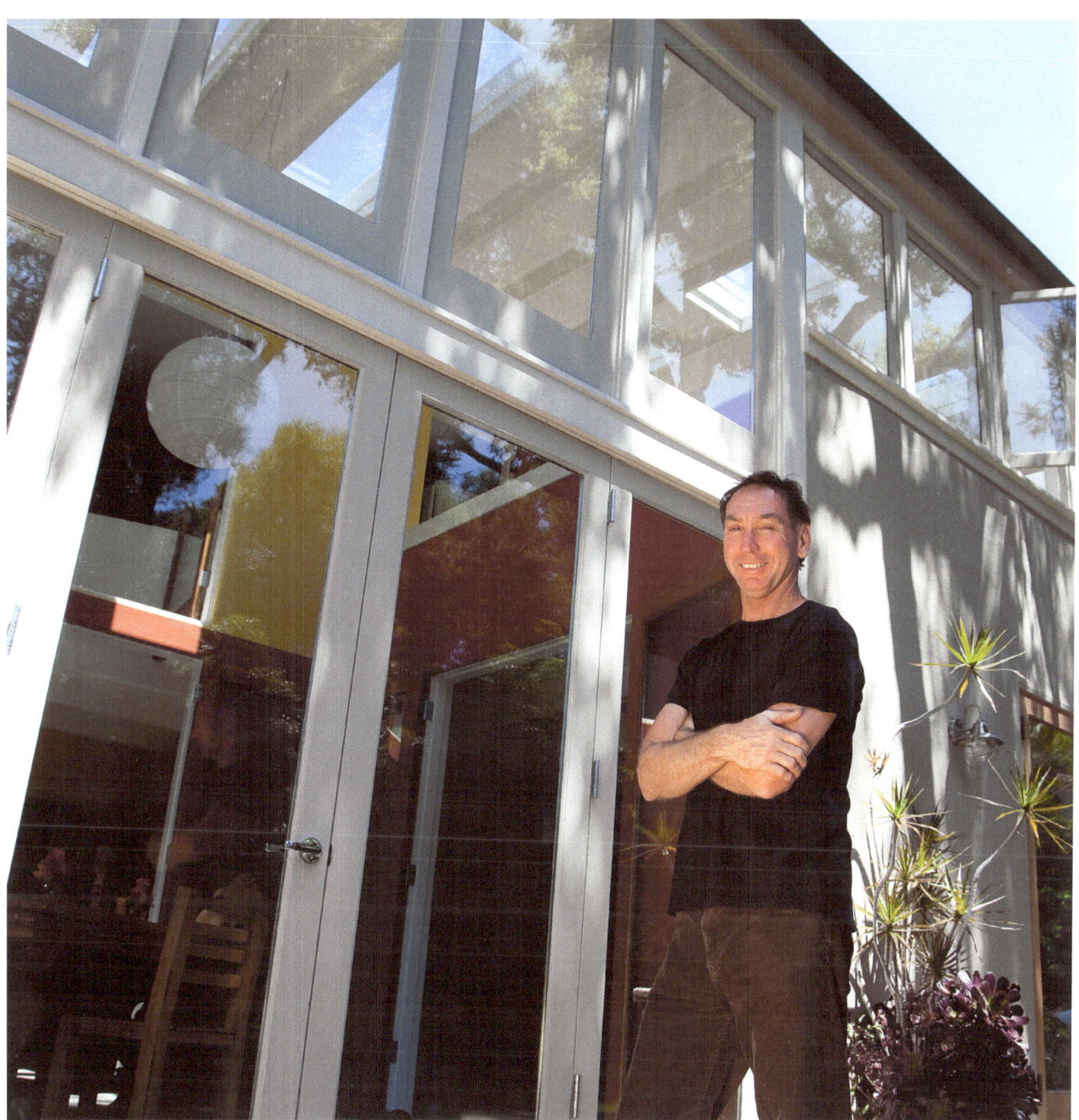

"It's your question to decide what reality you decide to invest your time in."

— Judy Goldhaft

JUDY GOLDHAFT AND PETER BERG
Planet Drum Foundation

Peter Berg was a visionary activist and pioneer in the environmental movement. He coined the term "bioregion", for a life-place with a distinct ecosystem and culture, often based around a watershed—a geographic terrain and a terrain of consciousness. Peter was publicly described as "a thorn of conscience in the City's ecological side."

Judy and Peter were part of the San Francisco Mime Troupe, and central to the San Francisco Diggers. The Diggers explored alternative social forms including free food, housing, medical care and education and ran a Free Store.

Berg founded and directed Planet Drum Foundation which provides an innovative voice for bioregional sustainability, education and culture. Through its projects, publications, speakers, performances, and workshops, the organization encourages local groups and individuals to find sustainable ways to live with the natural aspects of their life-places, and provides assistance to bioregionally oriented groups. It also works around the world to help integrate urban areas into their bioregions, encouraging sustainable green city development with both ideas and hands-on projects.

Goldhaft has produced and still performs theater pieces based on multispecies relationships and relationships with natural systems. She has also worked in a variety of capacities with Planet Drum Foundation.

Peter passed away on July 28th, 2011. Judy continues to run Planet Drum Foundation.

www.planetdrum.org

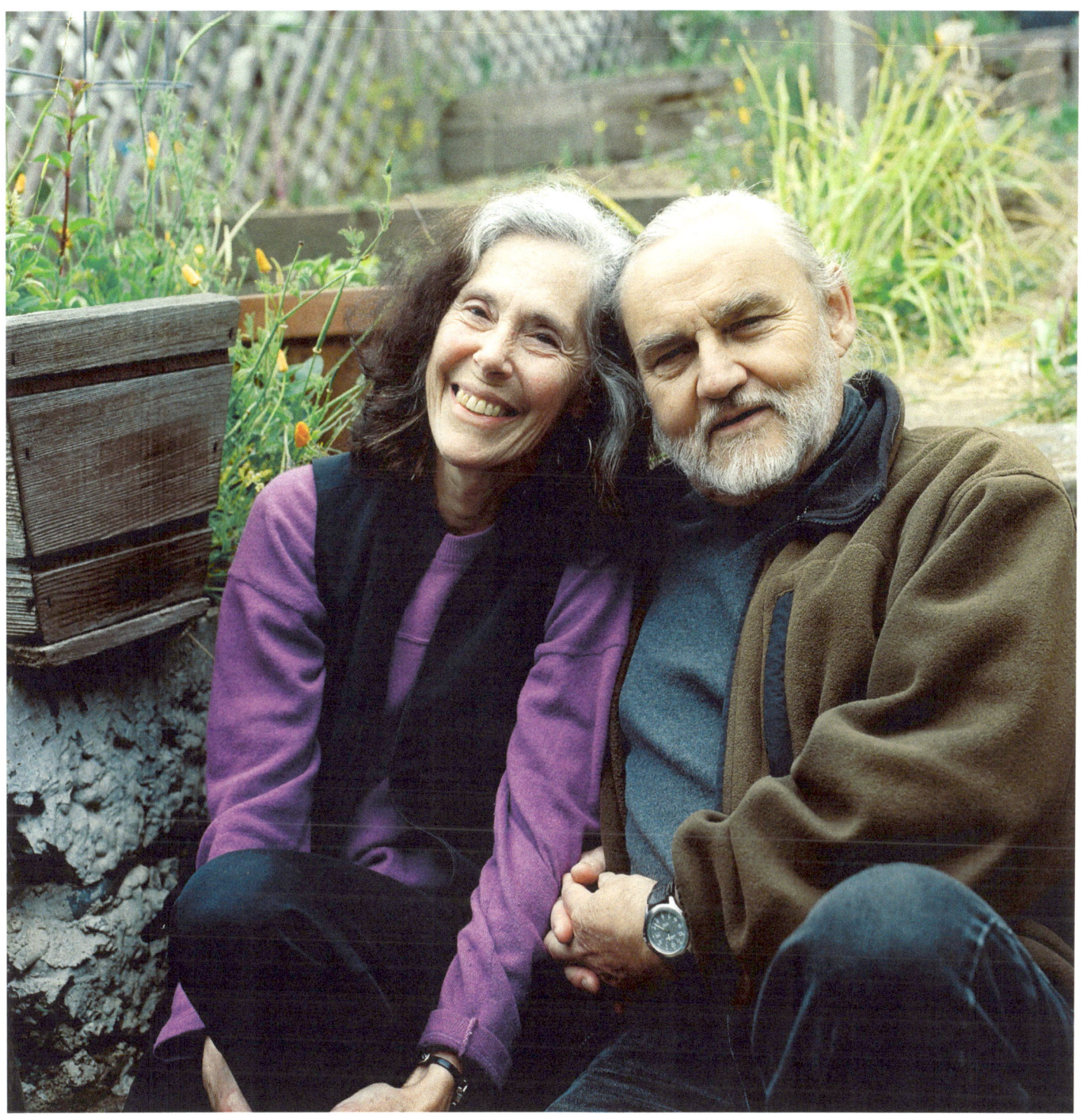

"There is a tremendous need to not only transform our consciousness about the relationship of people to nature, but to actually begin living a different kind of life that is geared toward blending with nature."

— Peter Berg

"Food forests are healthy ecosystems we create in cooperation with nature. They provide us with food, fiber, medicine and wood in a sustainable way. Food forests nurture nature, rather than destroying it. At a deep spiritual level being in a food forest reminds us of what we have often forgotten, that we always have been and always will be part of nature, and are deeply interconnected with all living things, indeed with the entire universe."

— Larry Saltzman

LARRY SALTZMAN AND LINDA BUZZELL SALTZMAN
Permaculture educators

Since Linda and Larry took a Permaculture Design Course in 2006, they've created a bountiful permaculture food forest in their backyard in Santa Barbara, California, with over 100 fruit trees plus vegetables, herbs and edible flowers on 1/3 acre. Larry serves as president of the Santa Barbara chapter of California Rare Fruit Growers, has designed a number of community food forests, and cares for over 300 fruit and nut trees. He teaches regular classes on "How to Create a Backyard Food Forest" and leads the "Mediterranean Food Forest" discussion group on Facebook.

A psychotherapist for over 30 years, Linda pioneers the new field of ecotherapy, which focuses on healing the human-nature relationship, on both individual and community levels. She and ecopsychology professor Craig Chalquist wrote *Ecotherapy: Healing with Nature in Mind* (Sierra Club Books, 2009), and they are currently completing a new book, *Cultural Resilience: An Integral Approach.* Linda teaches at Pacifica Graduate Institute in the MA/PhD Depth Psychology program in Community Psychology, Liberation Psychology and Ecopsychology, as well as the "Introduction to Ecoresilience" course at the California Institute of Integral Studies in San Francisco. She blogs for The Huffington Post on ecopsychology and ecotherapy.

They both worked for Captain Jacques Cousteau - Larry as a film editor and Linda as a development executive and Director of Research. They also worked for David L. Wolper Productions, which produced the National Geographic series. Linda founded the International Documentary Association (IDA), a professional association for nonfiction film and video makers.

www.EcoTherapyHeals.com
www.documentary.org

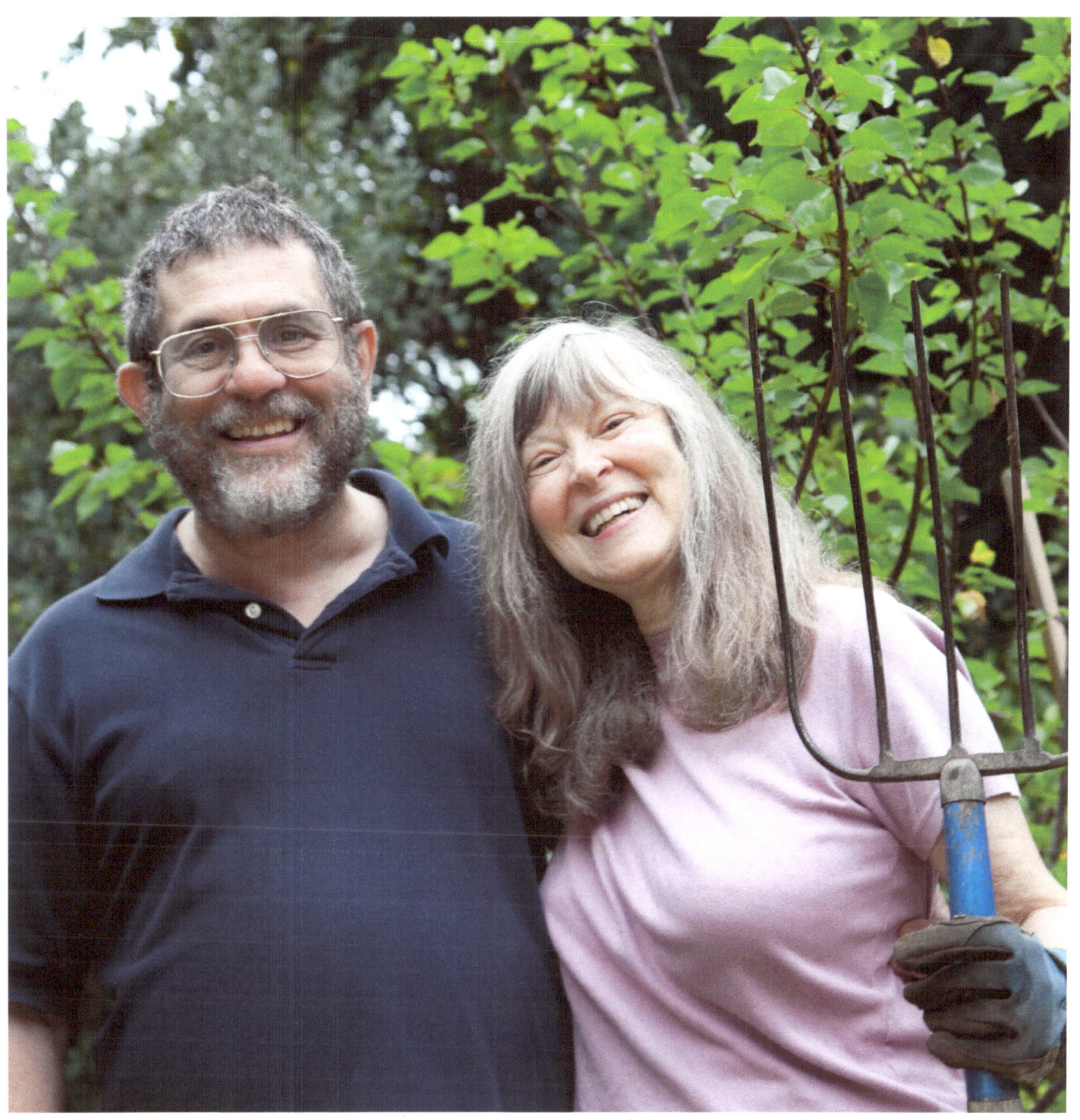

"In the modern world, so many of us long for a deep connection with the rest of nature that will fill the emotional and spiritual void caused by our destructive industrial lifestyles. We know we're missing something big, something wonderful – but it's hard to articulate what that is until we actually immerse ourselves again in the sacred aliveness of nature, our wild bodies and wild spirits, our relationship with other living beings on this planet and the universe that is our true home. At that point, we realize that what we've really been craving all along isn't more stuff or more drugs or more excitement or more time online: it's the bonding with all that is."

— Linda Buzzell Saltzman

"What is most needed to preserve environmental well-being is not more law; it's more love."

MARC MCGINNES
Pioneering environmental activist, attorney and educator

Marc McGinnes has been an innovative pioneer in the fields of public interest environmental advocacy, law and education since 1969, when he helped to organize the first Earth Day observances held in 1970.

He was a leading founder of the Community Environmental Council and the Environmental Defense Center, two Santa Barbara-based nonprofit organizations widely-respected for their work on a wide variety of local, state and national issues for over 40 years, and he was a founding member of the Environmental Studies Program at the University of California, Santa Barbara, where he developed and taught ten courses, including the nation's longest-running undergraduate course in environmental law and policy. The winner of numerous teaching awards, he incorporated into the curriculum lessons learned from his experience as one of the country's earliest practitioners of public interest environmental law.

At present he is retired from teaching and law practice and is engaged in a number of writing projects, including a book about practices of gratitude.

www.cecsb.org
www.environmentaldefensecenter.org
www.es.ucsb.edu/people/emeriti/j-marc-mcginnes

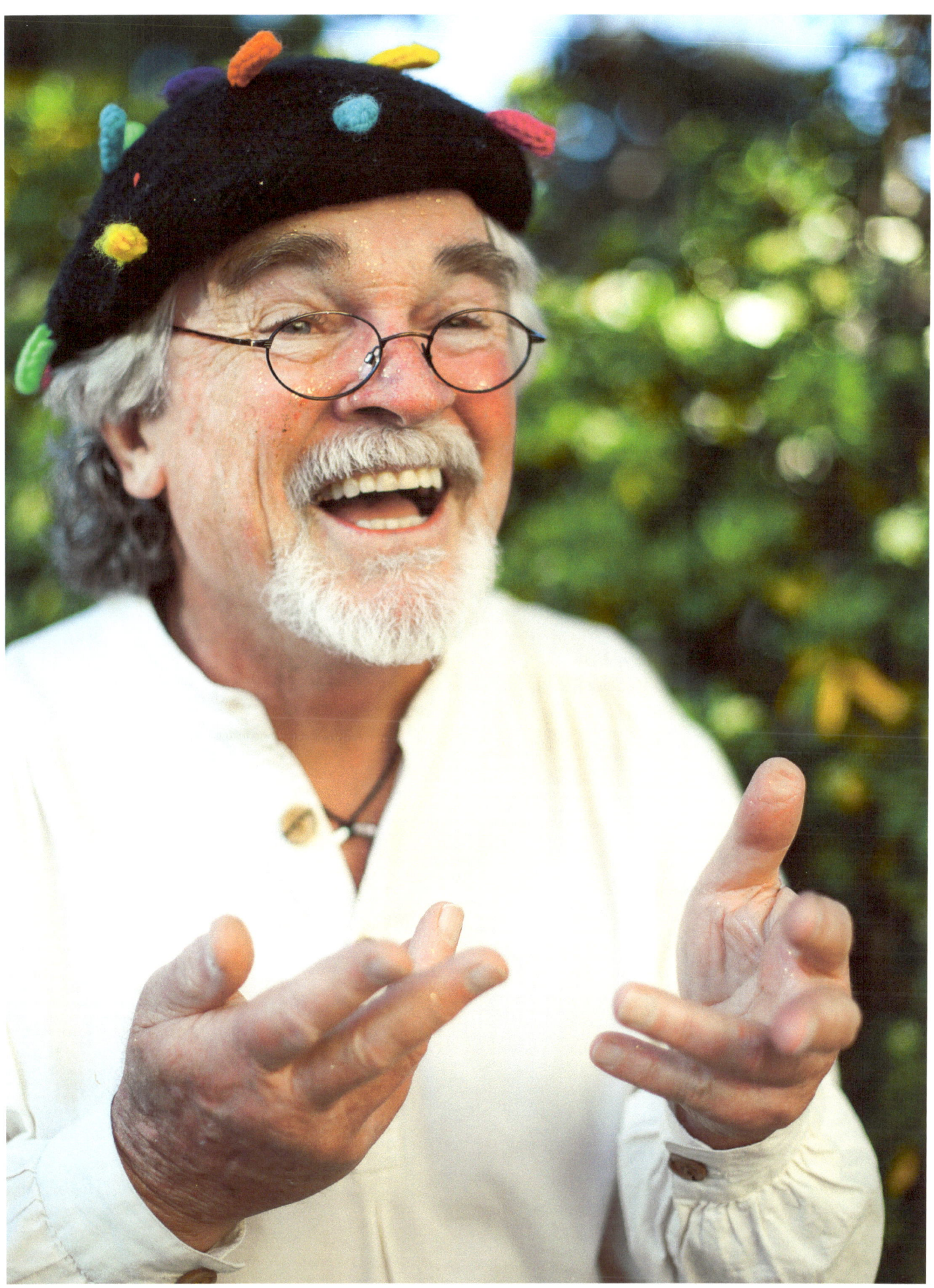

"Eat food. Not too much. Mostly plants."

MICHAEL POLLAN
Writer, professor

A Knight Professor of Journalism at UC Berkeley, the contributing writer to the New York Times Magazine and other publications has published numerous books, including *In Defense of Food: An Eater's Manifesto, The Omnivore's Dilemma: A Natural History of Four Meals, The Botany of Desire, Second Nature*, and *A Place of My Own.*

"Don't eat anything your great-grandmother wouldn't recognize as food," he likes to say, to illustrate that great-grandmothers never cooked with "edible food-like substances" such as guar gum, carrageenan, mono- and diglycerides, hydrolyzed vegetable protein, modified food starch, soy lecithin and other ingredients found in processed food. Michael Pollan is shifting our perception of what food is, back to locally grown, home-cooked and made with love; and this is truly delicious. Pollan teaches at UC Berkeley, and contributes to the Edible Schoolyard Project, a foundation dedicated to a "Delicious Revolution" in the school lunch curriculum, which includes gardening and farming education.

www.edibleschoolyard.org
www.michaelpollan.com

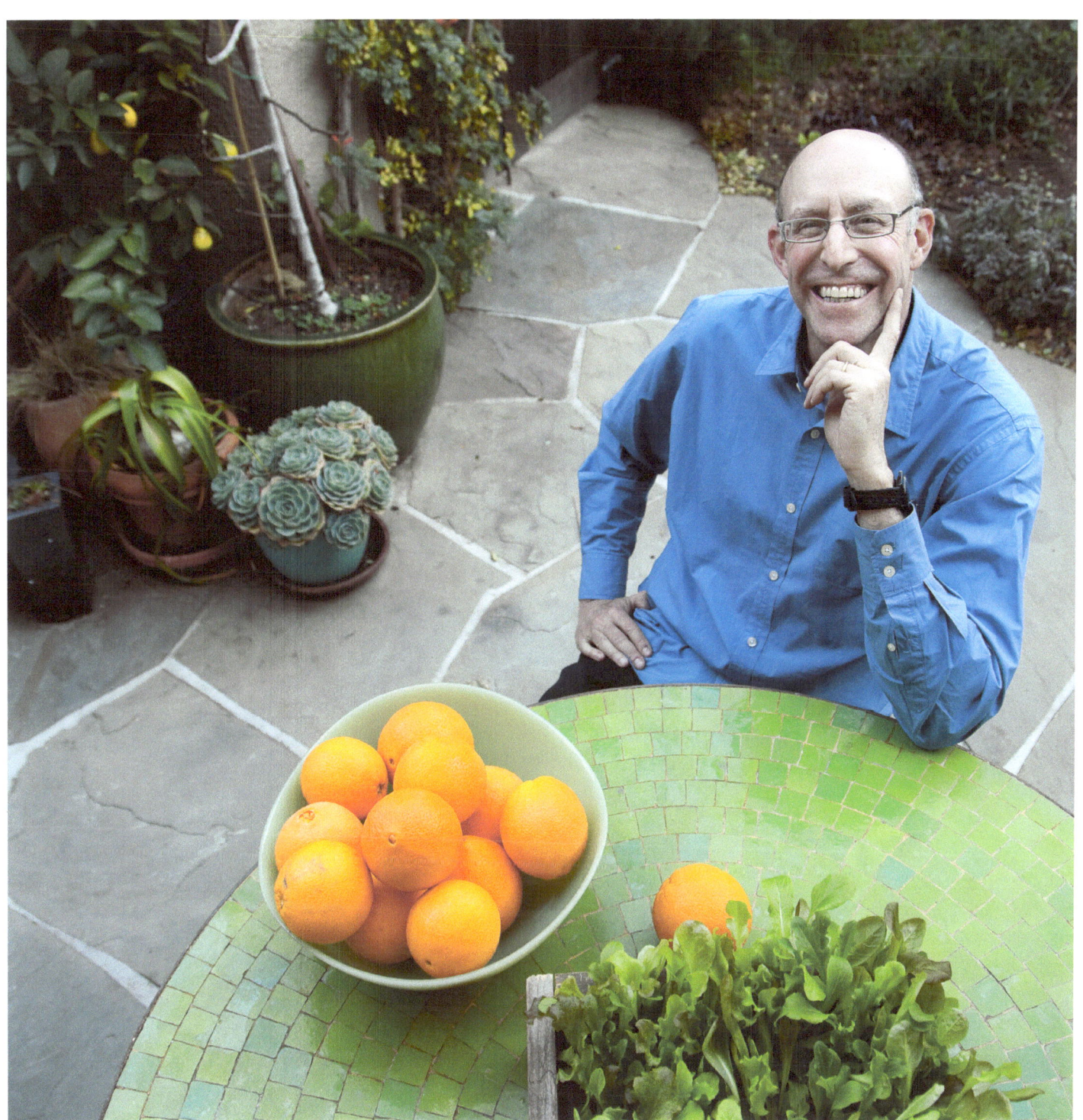

"The uprising of women's leadership —and elevating the feminine toward greater equilibrium within ourselves, our institutions and our cultures— is pivotal to this time when we must heal our relations with the web of life. Around the globe, peoples' economies, governance, human rights and equity, community resilience, peace and relationships to the health of our air, water and food are all being improved by greater women's involvement and initiatives. As a Maori leader and educator recently noted, 'We women will be essential toward shifting things, as we have an invisible umbilical cord connecting our bodies to our mother, the Earth.'"

— Nina Simons

NINA SIMONS AND KENNY AUSUBEL
Co-founders of Bioneers

Bioneers acts as a diverse forum of leading thinkers, doers and activists, and as a hub for networking, ideas and communications that promotes "breakthrough solutions and innovative social strategies for restoring Earth's imperiled ecosystems and healing our human communities". The group hosts the annual Bioneers Conference in the San Francisco Bay Area in October, a gathering for social and scientific innovators, students, teachers and anyone who wants to join the growing phenomenom.

They produce extensive media, including live-streamed webinars and conference seminars, an award-winning radio series, books and online media resources. The Bioneers are creating an active movement for a healthy, equitable, diverse and beautiful world, "our legacy for future generations."

www.bioneers.org

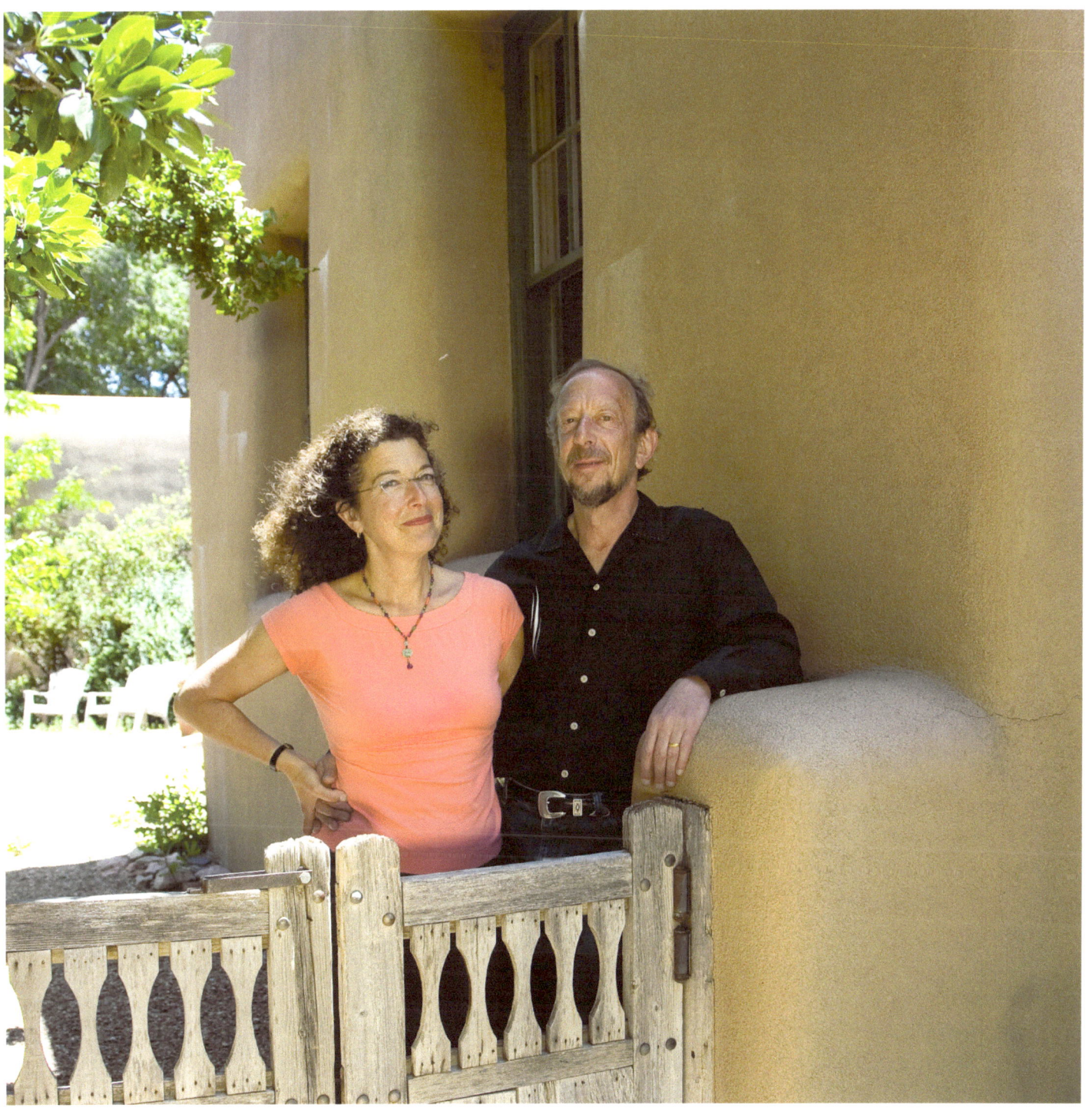

"The world is moving from breakdown to breakthrough. The coming years will be the most important years in the history of human civilization as 'the shift hits the fan.' We are called upon to reimagine civilization in the Age of Nature. It's wildly complex but not complicated. Taking care of nature means taking care of people – and taking care of people means taking care of nature. It's a Declaration of Interdependence that invokes a revolution from the heart of nature and the human heart."

— Kenny Ausubel

"Humanity, I would suggest, is the frontrunner of evolution. We are the most advanced form of life on this planet, and thus we have a responsibility. If it is a meaningless reality we live in, it is our responsibility to give it meaning, to inject meaning into it."

— From the unpublished *Essential Paolo Soleri*

PAOLO SOLERI
Architect, visionary

Paolo Soleri dedicated his life to reinventing the urban development model. After receiving his Ph.D. in Architecture in his native Italy at Torino Polytechnico in 1946, he moved to the United States to study with Frank Lloyd Wright. He was a pioneer in city design and a proponent for the car-less city as early as the 1960's.

He created his original studio, Cosanti, in Scottsdale, Arizona, and developed a wind bell crafting business to support his architectural endeavors. Later he began Arcosanti, in the desert of central Arizona, as a prototype for "arcology", putting theory into practice. Arcosanti, still under construction, continues the teachings of Paolo Soleri's ideas. Through arcology, cities are designed to maximize the interaction and accessibility of an urban environment, to minimize the use of energy, raw materials and land, reducing waste and environmental pollution, and to allow interaction with the surrounding natural environment.

His work has been exhibited worldwide, and he has written six books and numerous essays and monographs. Soleri also received a numer of prestigious fellowships, honorary doctorates, medals and awards, including the Golden Lion Award at La Bienale di Venizia in 2000. He was the subject of a major exhibition in Rome on his life and work, titled *Paolo Soleri: Ethics and Urban Inventiveness* in 2005.

www.arcosanti.org

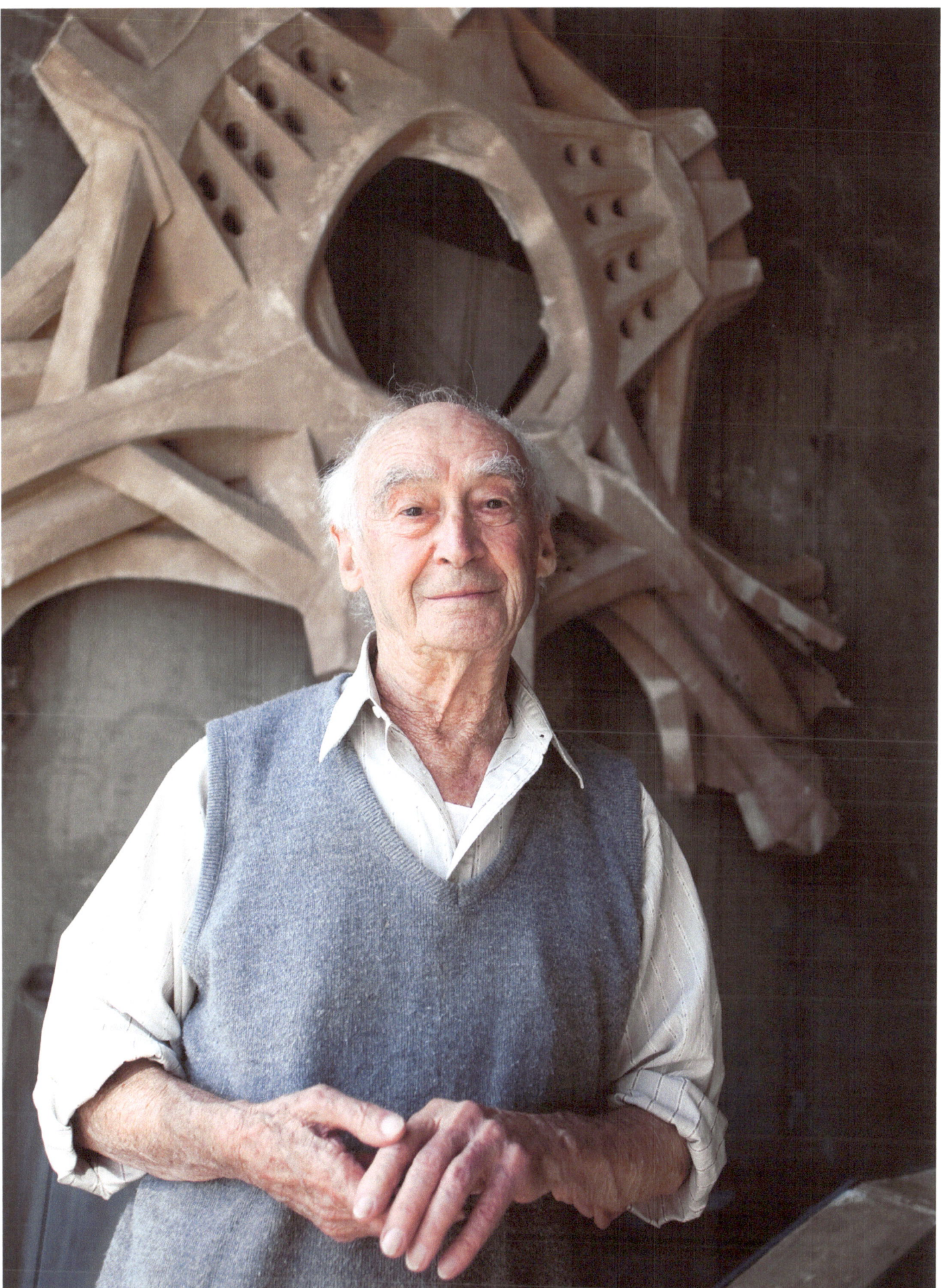

"There are many things we can do about the dilemmas we face, including limiting our population, being fair in consumption so that we redistribute resources properly, dealing with things we have to do to change our energy system to reduce the problems of climate change, dealing with toxic substances, protecting our fisheries, protecting biodiversity..."

PAUL EHRLICH
Writer, professor

Paul Ehrlich serves as President for the Center for Conservation Biology, a research and education organization within the Department of Biology at the College of William and Mary, providing information to enable conservation. Their information is used to determine which parcels of land warrant protection, how government policies should be written and implemented, and how vulnerable species should be managed.

He serves as Bing Professor of Population Studies at Stanford University, and has written many books, including *The Population Bomb* (1968), in which he warned about the dangers of overpopulation. Although his predictions were not entirely accurate, he did bring the idea of responsibility for global human population to light.

Most recently, he co-wrote, with his wife Anne H. Ehrlich, *The Dominant Animal: Human Evolution and the Environment.*

www.ccbbirds.org

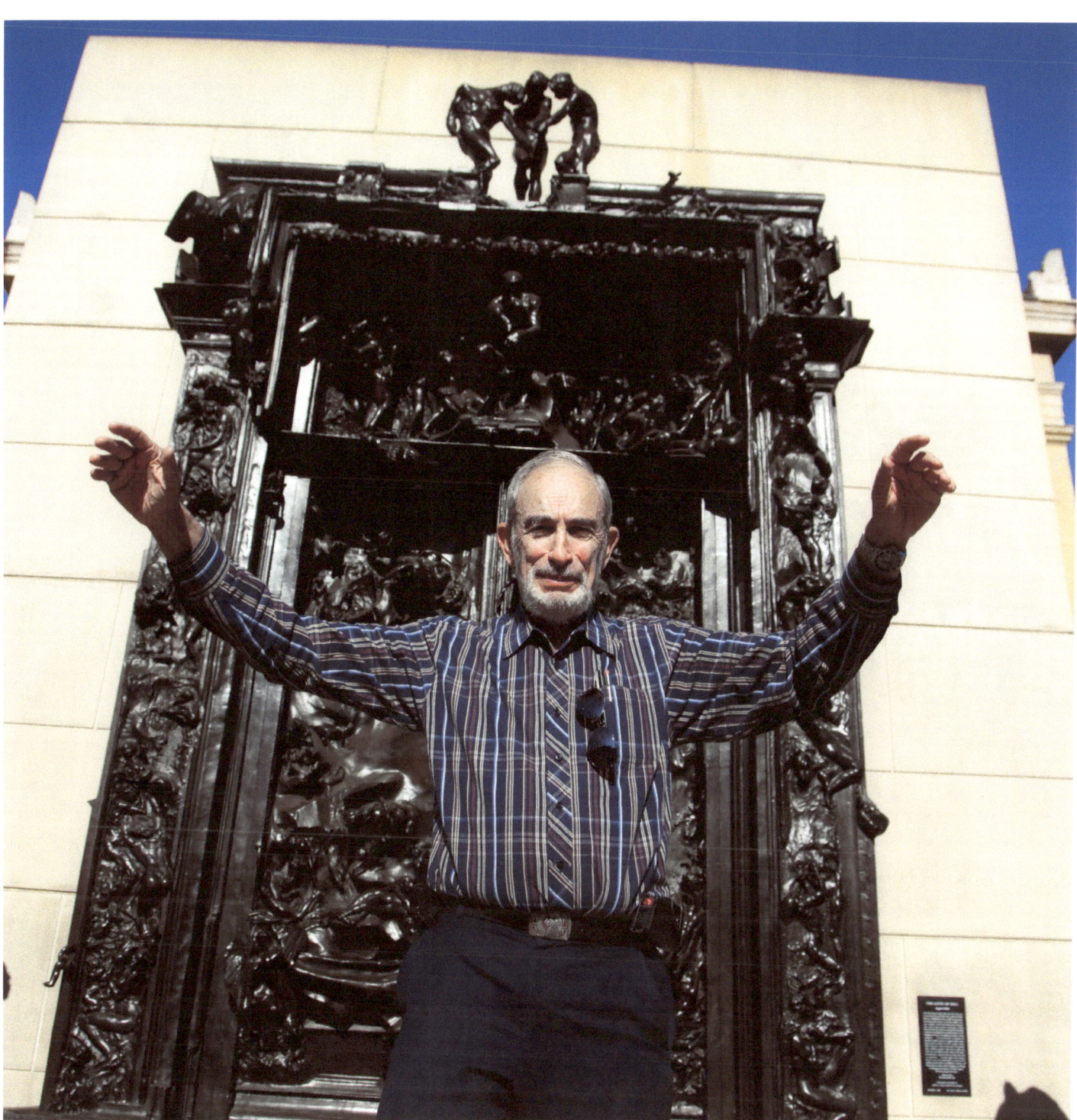

"The tools to take us out of the oil age are here."

PAUL RELIS
Co-founder of Community Environmental Council

Paul Relis was the founding Executive Director of the Community Environmental Council (CEC) of Santa Barbara for twenty years. The CEC was an outgrowth of the Santa Barbara Oil Spill of 1969; a seminal event in the birth of the modern environmental movement. The organization helped pioneer modern recycling and green building, and has sustained one of the nation's most successful Earth Day celebrations since the first Earth Day was held on April 22, 1970. The CEC's current focus is to move the Santa Barbara region off fossil fuels as a response to the climate change challenge.

Paul was appointed by the Governor of California as a member of the California Integrated Waste Management Board with oversight responsibilities for the nation's most ambitious recycling and composting program, where he served until 1998, when he became Senior Vice President at CR&R, one of the nation's leading privately held waste management companies, where he's working on the development of post-landfill technology to convert municipal organic waste to renewable natural gas, a zero-carbon fuel; particularly in a anaerobic digestion facility in Riverside County that will produce enough renewable natural gas to power nearly 300 heavy duty waste and recycling trucks and divert 300,000 tons per year or organic waste now going to landfill.

Paul recently completed a 16-year lectureship at the University of California, Santa Barbara, and is in the process of finishing his book: *Out of the Wasteland: Stories from the Environmental Frontier* chronicling 40-years of pioneering work aimed at moving out of the oil age.

www.cecsb.org

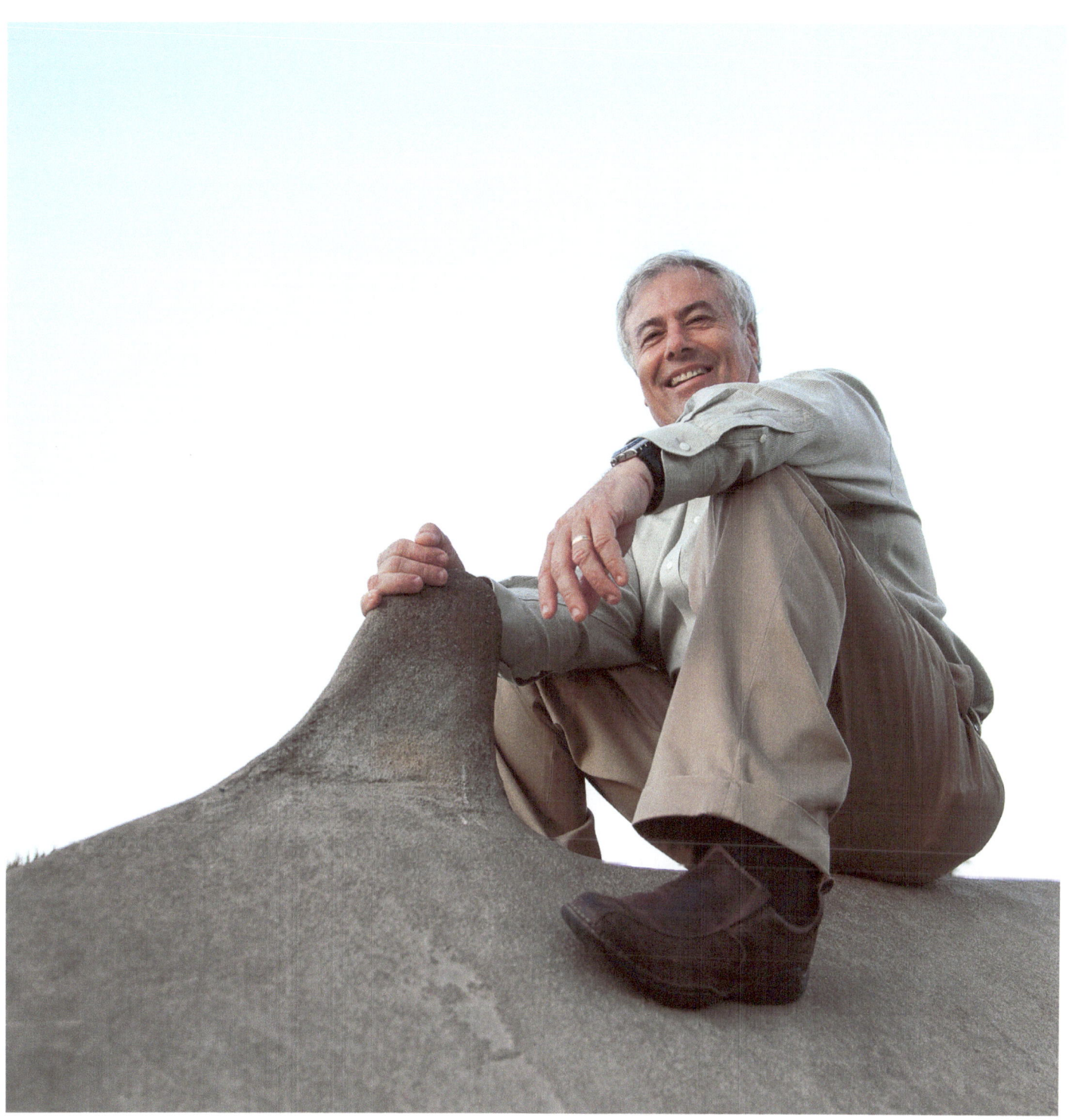

"By celebrating our Earth with others through outdoor experiences in nature, we honor life in a way that is joyful and meaningful and connects to the spirit of all life. Teaching the interconnection of all life is key to sustainability."

ROBERTA SALAZAR
Wildlife biologist, founder of Rivers and Birds

In 1998, Roberta Salazar established Rivers and Birds as a nonprofit organization to provide experiential education, "celebrating the interconnection of all life, and inspiring individuals to be leaders for Earth stewardship and peace." Their hands-on Watershed Learning Project is presented yearly to over five hundred fifth grade students in New Mexico. They also offer workshops, organize the Wild Film Festival and the Eco Film Series, and provide broad ecological research experience and data analysis expertise to local, state, and federal land managers.

www.riversandbirds.org

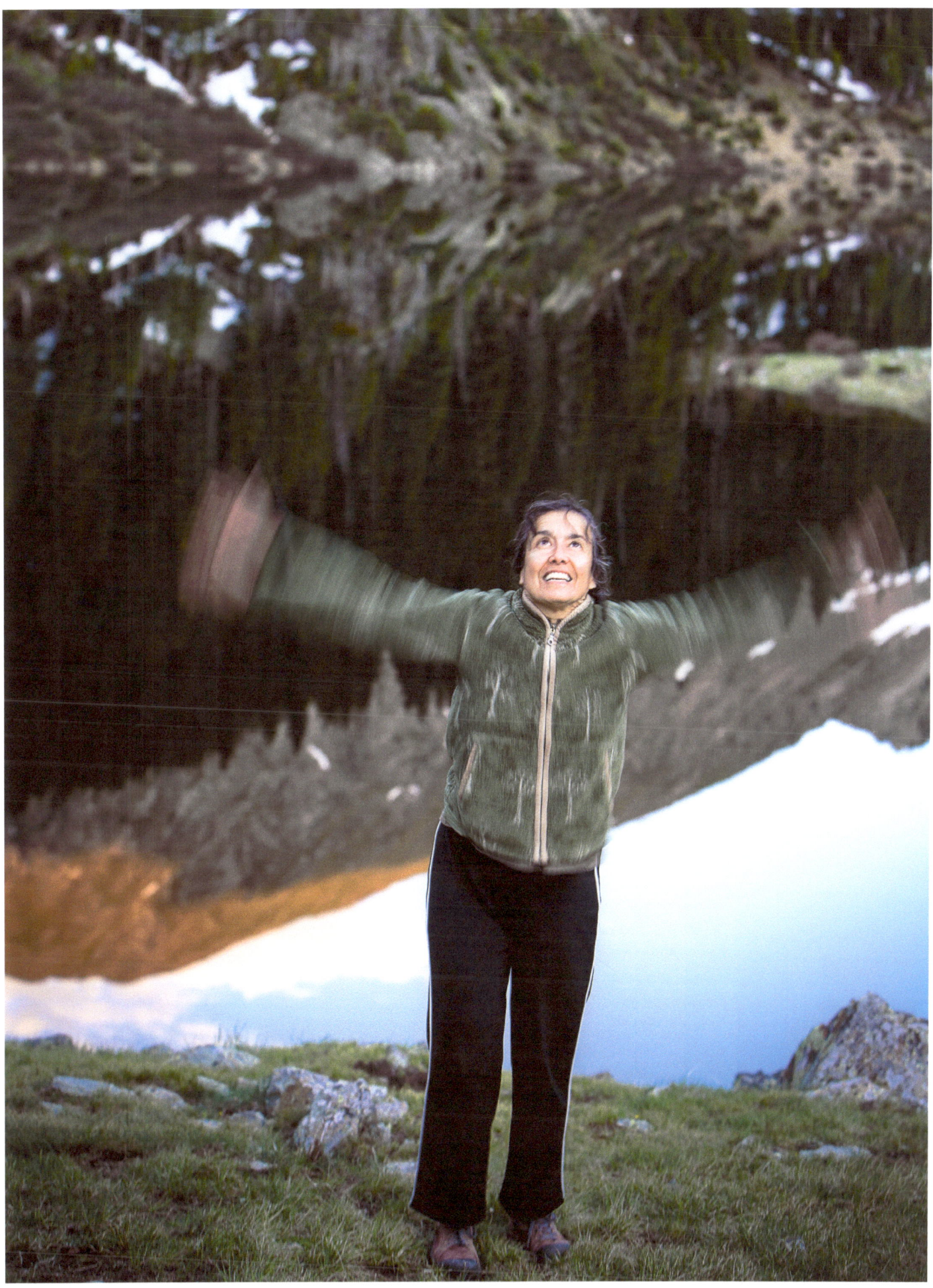

"We should live our lives so that we make a difference. Money is only good for the good you can do with it."

SELMA RUBIN
Activist, co-founder of Earth Day

Selma Rubin, environmental activist and mother of a movement, helped preserve the Gaviota coastline, among other major accomplishments. In 1970, she and a small group stopped a proposed development of 1,535 homes in this beautiful canyon. Today, much of it has been put into a conservation easement with the Land Trust for Santa Barbara County, protecting and preserving it forever (although some properties remain in jeopardy). The ballot initiative she promoted and ultimately won (and for which she was nearly jailed), kept the California coastline undeveloped from Goleta to north of Gaviota. It was before the California Coastal Commission existed, and before California environmental law had been drafted.

During over 50 years of continual grassroots involvement, Rubin, a bookkeeper, helped spawn or guide at least 42 groups and organizations, including the Community Environmental Council (CEC), the Environmental Defense Center (EDC), PUEBLO, the League of Conservation Voters, Santa Barbara County Action Network (SB CAN), the Santa Barbara Women's Political Committee, the Fund for Santa Barbara, and the Homeless Coalition. She remained actively on a number of boards until her passing, at age 96.

Selma was a midwife for Earth Day, and grandmother to a generation of organizations and activists worldwide for the environment, human rights and social justice. She passed away on March 9, 2012.

www.cecsb.org
www.edcnet.org
www.fundforsantabarbara.org
www.sbpueblo.org
www.lcv.org
www.sbcan.org

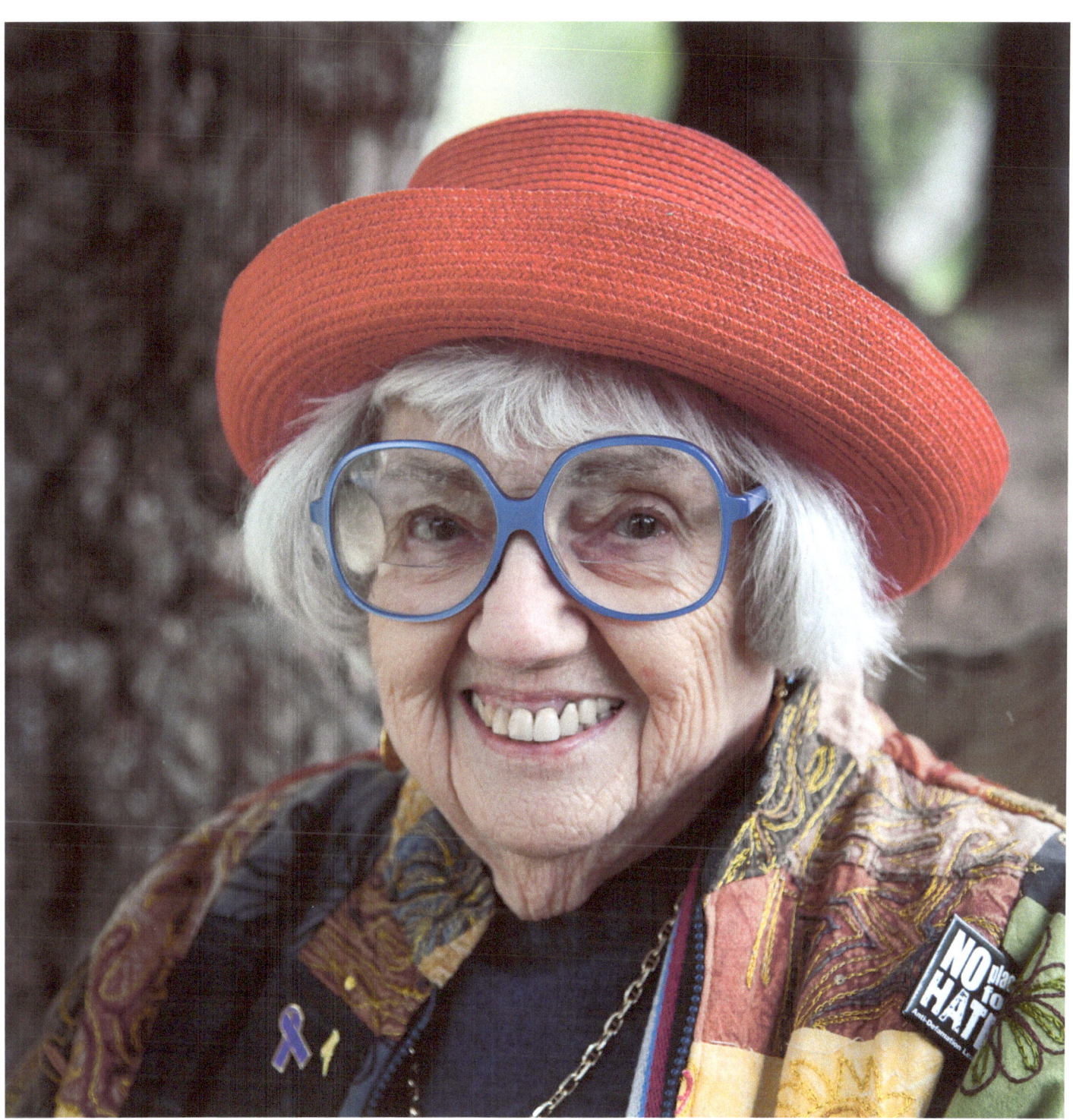

"All the damage we cause to the oceans we cause to ourselves."

SYLVIA EARLE
Oceanographer

Dr. Sylvia Earle, oceanographer and author of numerous books, including *The Blue Planet, Oceans* and others, is a pioneer in ocean exploration and research and is currently an Explorer-in-Residence at the National Geographic Society, leader of the Sustainable Seas Expeditions, chair of the Advisory Councils for Harte Research Institute and for the Ocean in Google Earth. Dr. Earle also served as Chief Scientist of NOAA in the early 1990s, and received the coveted TED Prize in 2009 for her proposal to establish a global network of marine protected areas.

She convinced Google to include maps of the oceans in Google Earth. As a three-year-old, she was swept off her feet by a wave, and a long-lasting love affair began. Now she dedicates her life to protecting our oceans.

www.mission-blue.org

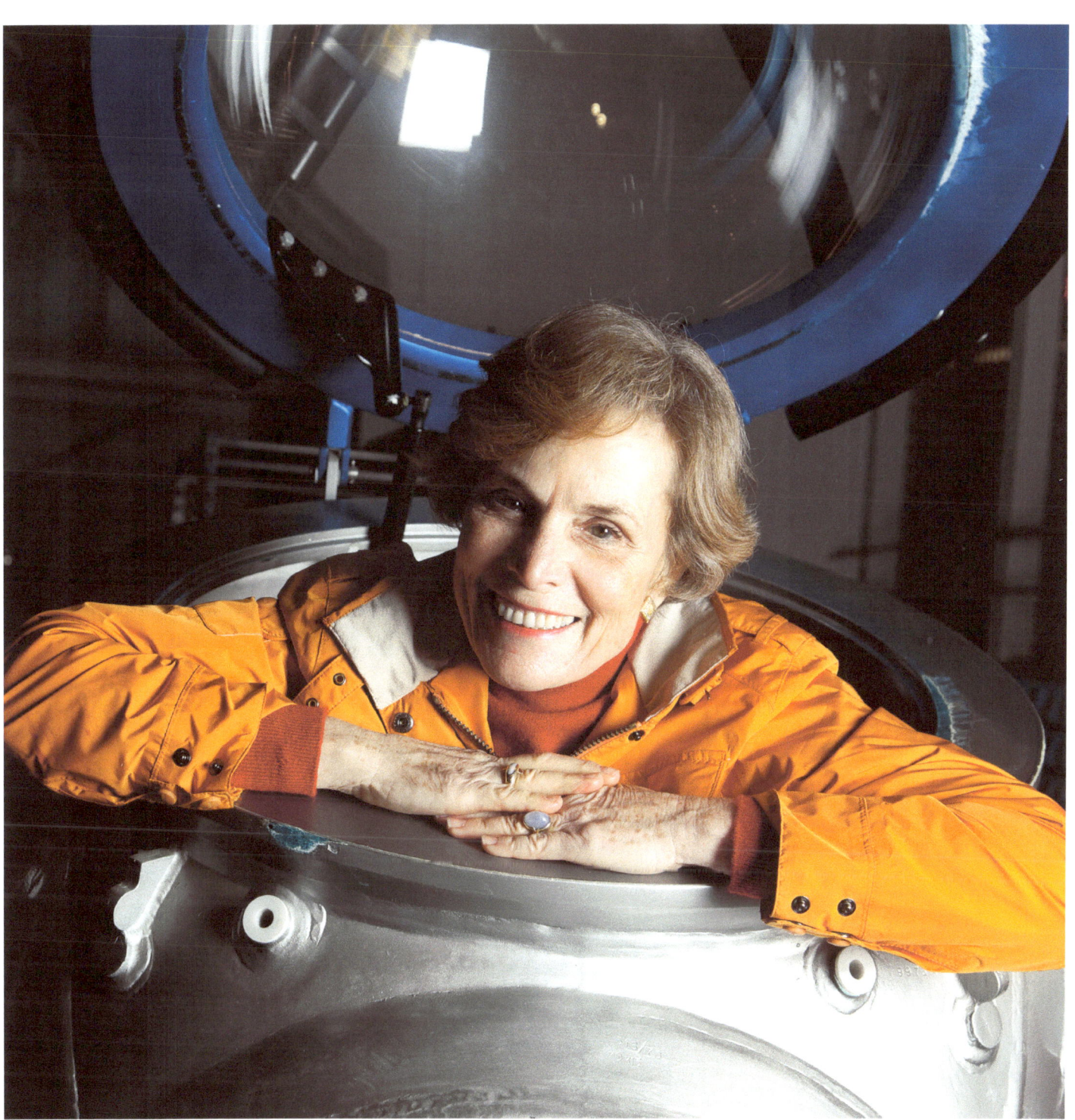

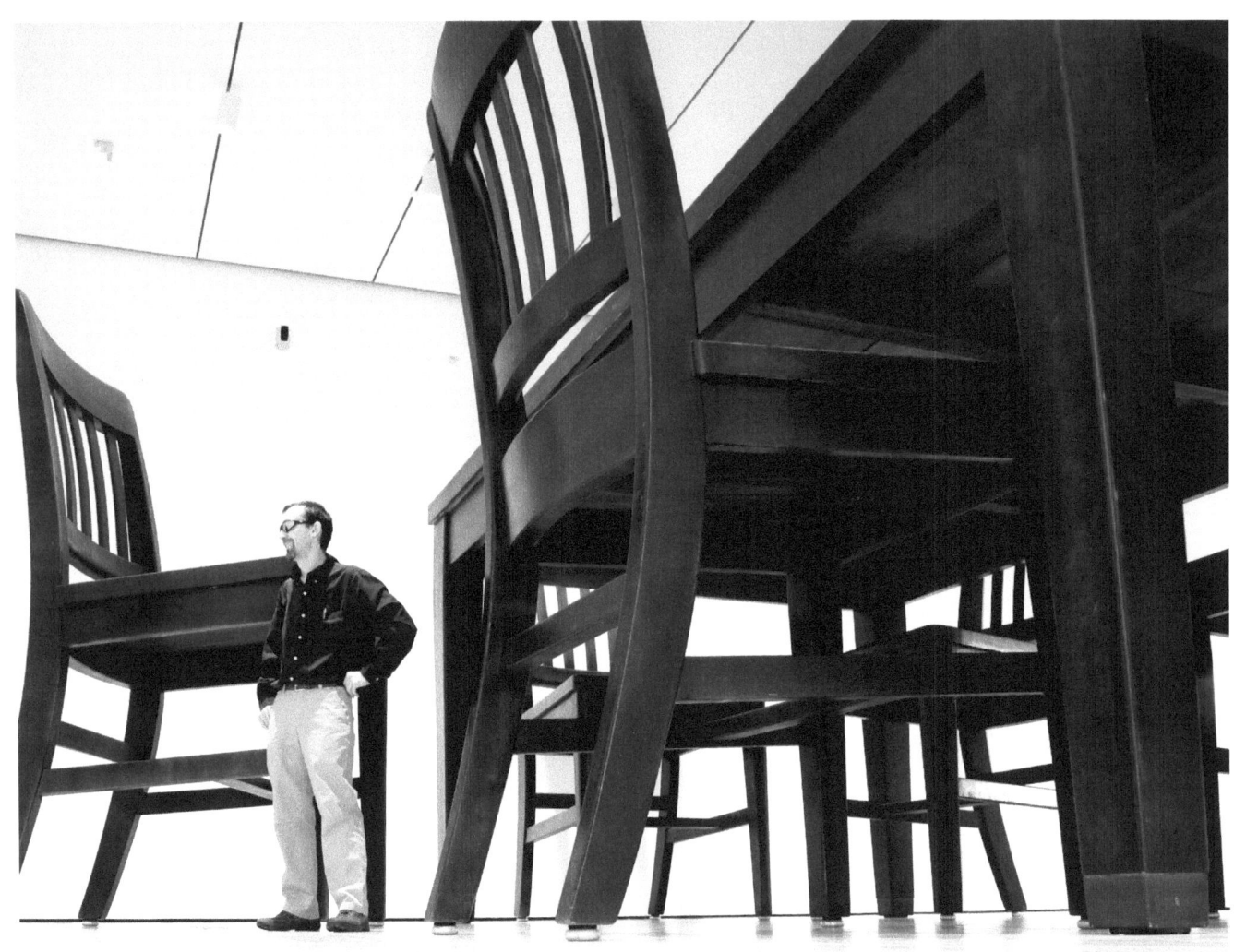

ISAAC HERNÁNDEZ
Photographer, Writer, Painter, Sculptor
Self-Portrait with "Under the Table" by Robert Therien. LACMA, Los Angeles, California, 2008

www.isaachernandez.com

PHOTOGRAPHER'S BIO

ISAAC HERNÁNDEZ
Madrid, Spain, 1967

Isaac Hernández carries on a family tradition of photography began by his great-great-grandfather Luis Tarszenski, the Count of Lipa, who learned the art of the daguerrotype from Louis-Jacques-Mandé Daguerre. Tarszenski introduced photography to the south of Spain, where years later Isaac's father, Enrique Hernández "Luike", began a career as a photojournalist, publisher, caricaturist and nationally-awarded poet.

Isaac studied Geography and History at the Universidad Complutense in Madrid before earning a Bachelor of Arts in Photography and Film from Brooks Institute of Photography. He continues his studies, and is near completion of an Associate of Arts degree in Studio Arts from Santa Barbara City College.

He co-founded Mercury Press International in 1991, a media services company committed to publishing articles and photographs of excellence, integrity and inspiration. His photographs and words have appeared in over 300 titles in 27 countries, including *Art, El Mundo, Focus, Geo, Glamour, National Geographic Traveler, Sports Illustrated for Kids, Stern, USA Today* and *The Wall Street Journal*. He's currently working on several books, including a collection of photographic profiles of EcoHeroes.

Isaac has directed several short films and animations, including *The Bees* (1989), and has written and produced four plays in collaboration with children: *The Bridge to Nowhere* (2003), *The Last Play on Earth: No Child Left Behind* (2010), *The End of Rainbows* (2011), and *The Magical Seaweed* (2012), directing the last three.

Currently he's creating an oil pastel a day, with the goal of exhibiting all 365 paintings in one show. His work enriches many international collections, and he's a member of the Madrid-based artist collective La Mosca en el Reloj. Isaac also teaches art and photography, and has lectured at Brooks Institute of Photography and at the Universidad Complutense in Madrid.

MAJOR EXHIBITS AND AWARDS

2014
Daily Paintings: The First Four Months. Solo Exhibit. Roy, Santa Barbara.

2013
Invited Artist, Santa Clarita Art Slam.

2012
I'm Not My Face: 40 Years of Self-Portraits. Solo Exhibit. Roy, Santa Barbara.

2010-11
EcoHeroes. Solo Exhibit. 40th Anniversary Santa Barbara Earth Day and SB Channels.

2009
Difference Makers. Solo Exhibit. Samy's Camera Gallery, Santa Barbara.

Collective Works. Atkinson Gallery, Santa Barbara. Merit Award for sculpture *Fifteen Seconds*.

Circles. Art from Scrap Gallery, Santa Barbara.

2008
Collective Works. Atkinson Gallery, Santa Barbara.

2007
My Home in a Lima Shanty Town. Solo Exhibit. Santa Barbara Art Studios.

En un Mundo Nuevo y Feliz. Madrid, Spain.

1990
Santa Barbara, Collaborative Mural. Santa Barbara Museum of Art, Santa Barbara.

World Travel. SB Expo. Second and Third Prize.

Brooks Institute of Photography Excellence Award.

1988
Paintings and Photographs in Black-and-White. Solo Exhibit. Sienna Gallery, Santa Barbara.

Collective Works. Brooks Institute. Second Prize.

1987
Spain. Solo Exhibit. Roma Gallery, Santa Barbara.

1985
United States. First and Third Prize. Washington Irving Institute, Madrid.

www.ingramcontent.com/pod-product-compliance
Lightning Source LLC
Chambersburg PA
CBHW051200220526
45473CB00003B/851